PRAISE FOR *HEKATE: GODDESS OF WITCHES*

"With insight growing from roots in history and tradition, and a voice unafraid to share personal experience, Courtney Weber uses these keys to open the gate to the mystery that is Hekate. She is an excellent guide to help the reader develop their own relationship to the Goddess of Witches as she shares her own beautiful journey with Hekate." —Christopher Penczak, cofounder of the Temple of Witchcraft and author of *The Mighty Dead* and *The Outer Temple of Witchcraft*

"Hekate is a Goddess whose interaction with humans spans many centuries, many cultures, and nations. She is both the center and the circumference, the crossroads of liminality and the soul of the world, and despite a myriad of epithets she is not contained in any name. It is a bold and risky thing to try to describe her in a book. To do so is to invite Hekate's close scrutiny. Having read Courtney Weber's *Hekate: Goddess of Witches*, I believe that it pleases Hekate. This book is deeply personal, scholarly, practical, entertaining, sobering, and given as a heartfelt invitation to those who seek Hekate. It is a book for witches, those who would be witches, and for those trying to find their way back to their magick. It is a book that does not tell you what to do, but, like Hekate, it lights a torch, gives you the keys, and nudges you out to find your own way." —Ivo Dominguez Jr., author of *The Four Elements of the Wise* and *Spirit Speak*

"Hekate is the perfect crossroads where three different roads meet: historical, mythological, and magickal. Courtney Weber preserves the rich and often confusing history of this complex multi-named, many-faced deity, while also incorporating her into a practical and modern witchcraft practice. Throughout these pages, you will learn how to connect, honor, and petition the ancient torch-bearing Titaness of witchery with beautifully crafted and soul-stirring spells and prayers." —Mat Auryn, author of *Psychic Witch*

"Courtney Weber's lovingly produced *Hekate* does not merely discuss the Goddess of Witches. It also speaks to what her worship entails and how rewarding that worship is. This book features the words of modern priestesses as well as those from ancient sources. Hekate is found in liminal spaces: if you hear the call of the torch, the key, the dog, or the moon, you'll learn how to answer that call within these pages." —Amy Blackthorn, priestess of Hekate and author of *Blackthorn's Botanical Magic*

"I absolutely love this book! Courtney Weber has done an exceptional job of bringing us into the world of Hekate, Key Keeper and Goddess of the Crossroads, who opens doors, guards, and protects with her black dogs. Now, if I choose to work with her, I have a solid foundation upon which to build a loving, respectful, and sincere relationship with her. A new way to enter into the Crossroads of Magick." —Najah Lightfoot, author of *Good Juju*

"From ancient temples to modern altars, Hekate is a goddess whose worship has stood the test of time. In *Hekate*, Courtney Weber guides us to a new crossroads where the paths of history and Courtney's own personal experience intersect with our own. You do not have to be a witch to find the truth in these pages. Courtney's deep devotion to Hekate and "sacred casual" writing style make this sometimes intimidating and elusive goddess accessible to us all." —Melody Wingfield, creator of *The WitchQueen Project* podcast

"Courtney Weber delivers a haunting and powerful portrayal of Hekate for readers of all experience levels that is well researched and full of personal insight. Even after twenty-plus years of working with this beloved goddess, I found new information that I was able to add immediately to my practice, and that makes this book worth its weight in gold." —Devin Hunter, author of *The Witch's Book of Spirits*

HEKATE

HEKATE

Goddess of Witches

COURTNEY WEBER

WEISER BOOKS

This edition first published in 2021 by Weiser Books, an imprint of
Red Wheel/Weiser, LLC
With offices at:
65 Parker Street, Suite 7
Newburyport, MA 01950
www.redwheelweiser.com

ISBN: 978-1-57863-716-4
Library of Congress Cataloging-in-Publication Data available upon request.

Cover and interior design by Kathryn Sky-Peck
Cover art © Wojciech Zwoliński/Cambion Art
Hekate illustration © Laura Tempest Zakroff
Typeset in Arno Pro

Printed in the United States of America
IBI
10 9 8 7 6 5 4 3 2 1

"Hekate" by Laura Tempest Zakroff

For Sarah, Tamrha, and Wilson: my keys to Hekate

For to this day, whenever any one of men on earth offers rich sacrifices and prays for favor according to custom, he calls upon Hecate. Great honor comes full easily to him whose prayers the goddess receives favorably, and she bestows wealth upon him; for the power surely is with her.

—HESIOD, 700 BCE[1]

CONTENTS

Meeting Hekate

Triple Hecate, you who know all our undertakings,
and come, to aid the witches' art, and all our incantations.
—OVID, *METAMORPHOSES*

I was deep into a hot and lonely summer when I met Hekate. Nineteen years old and desperate to get out of town, I'd taken an unpaid apprenticeship at a theater company as far on the opposite coast as I could go. But it was my first time away from home, and I struggled with surprising homesickness. In my spare time, trying to fill hard, isolated hours, I read my first Witchcraft book. I was enthralled. For the first time, I found a label that described me: someone who spoke with spirits, had prophetic dreams, and found more of the divine at the ocean than in a church. I was a Witch. Many traditions of Witchcraft, I quickly learned, involved devotion to a goddess. But I didn't know what that meant. It scared me a little.

The meeting happened after a cast party. I wasn't feeling very social—at least not for human companionship, anyway. I walked outside with a plastic glass of wine. I don't recall if the moon was full, a quarter, or a sliver, but I remember that something on that dark, sticky night felt different. It was as though the moon looked right at me, perhaps as if it had been waiting for me.

I raised my wine to the moon and said, "Okay. I'm yours."

It's the simple moments that really change us. I didn't know it then, but I was meeting Hekate—the goddess of the crossroads, of the moon, of ghosts and crops, and of Witches.

In the nearly twenty years since that unassuming but powerful night, I've honored Hekate in rituals both intimate and packed. I've sought her to bless deceased loved ones, and sung her songs when euthanizing beloved pets. I prayed to her in the thin hours of the morning when our new, frightened puppy howled. I have ordained two priestesses dedicated to this strange and wonderful goddess, and have witnessed how she has transformed their lives.

She is known as a goddess of death, one who guards souls in the underworld, whose symbols include the black dog, the whip, and the dagger. She is known as the keeper of the crossroads, a goddess who helps those experiencing transition. She is called the key holder or torchbearer, the one who opens doors and reveals secrets, a goddess of the cosmos who holds mysteries beyond our modern understanding. She is associated with the depths of the sea, the stars of the night, and the fertile earth. She is a patroness of parents. She has also been called "the three-headed," "the one who arms the hand with murky, dreadful lamps," "goddess of the crossroads," "the voice of dogs," and "the far-darter." She has been associated with the underworld and mystical rites involving bloody sacrifices, justice, and creatures of revenge.

She has been many things over millennia, but to both ancient devotees and those of the modern age, Hekate is the goddess of Witches.

In my own journey, Hekate has remained a consistent background presence—one I appreciated but didn't give much thought outside of periodic devotions. But the most recent chapter in my Witchcraft journey involved a crossroads.

Let me take a step back.

A couple of years after I raised that glass of wine to the moon, I moved to New York City for a theater career, but also to pursue my new spirituality. It was difficult to explore the newly found Witchy part of myself in a community that knew me as Catholic Courtney.

In New York, I was taken at my word. If I said I was a Witch, no one smirked. In an enormous, busy city, I could proudly flaunt my pentacle necklace. Few people seemed to care, and those who did genuinely appreciated that part of me. It didn't take me long to find many like-minded people. Within a few years, I was running one of the largest Witchcraft communities in the tri-state area. I was enthralled. Not only was I able to be the person I'd wanted to be, but also I had created the spiritual community I'd once hoped to find. Witchcraft blessed my life immensely. It led me to travel and write, helping me manifest a childhood dream of being an author. It also led me to meet the love of my life, who is himself a Witch. Witchcraft gave meaning and agency to my life in a way that the religion of my youth never had.

It was through this Witchcraft journey that I came to know Hekate: a formidable force, but also a comforting and healing one. She was the goddess who inspired some of the smartest, most compassionate Witches I knew. She was a never-ending puzzle, with each new story, myth, or attribute creating an even more beautiful but complicated story—one I never got tired of hearing. She appealed to the brilliant cross-section of cultures and practices that made up the New York Witchcraft community I loved.

I had dedicated two books to other goddesses I loved but was at a crossroads of what to do with myself. I was no longer leading a community. It was time to write another book, but on what?

Through a series of signs and dreams, and synchronicity, it became clear. Hekate had touched my life in so many beautiful and profound ways. It was time I wrote a book for her.

WHO IS HEKATE?

Like many goddesses of the Old World, Hekate's origins are mysterious. She is commonly known as a goddess of ancient Greece, a period which is generally understood to encompass 1200 BCE–500 CE, but she did not originate there. She may have originated in the Minoan civilization (2700–1100 BCE), or was at least influenced by gods of that culture. Evidence of Hekate worship has also been found in Sicily, Libya, Turkey, Bulgaria, and Syria. One of the earliest records of Hekate in Thrace is from Abdera, a sixth-century colony in what is now Turkey. The Turkish town of Lagina is thought to be home to her most important cult center.[1] In ancient Rome (800 BCE to roughly 500 CE), she was given many complimentary titles, including "savior," "greatest," and "most manifest."[2] The first writer to describe her was the poet Hesiod, who lived in ancient Greece between 750 and 650 BCE and wrote about Hekate as though she was already quite familiar—not only to himself but to his contemporaries, too, hinting that we are looking at a very ancient goddess indeed. Hekate is described in the myths as being older than the other gods, and sometimes as coming from an unspecified, faraway place.

Hekate owns a shifting but ever-present role among the Greek gods. She is believed to have been worshipped among the oldest of the gods of Olympus and was even considered an equal to the Olympian king Zeus.[3] One inscription from the Roman Imperial period (27 BCE–476 CE) states that Hekate was so great that in order to obtain priesthood of Hekate, one must obtain priesthood of Zeus.[4] Hekate is first described as a Titan, one of the great giants of the universe whom Zeus overthrew. But instead of fighting Zeus, as many

Titans did, she joined his campaign, helping tear down the old way to make space for the new.

Although she did not originate in ancient Greece, Hekate is most often associated with this culture and time period. To better understand Hekate, it may prove helpful to look at how the ancient Greeks honored their gods. Their religion was a combination of reverence and fear for gods who lived on high on Mount Olympus. These gods could appear to the mortal people, tricking them (or taking them), even marrying or mating with them. Religious rites of this period were tied to the cycles of the harvest, life and death, all connected to the complex identities of the gods they worshipped. Religious life in ancient Greece was accentuated by mystery cults, maintained by priests and priestesses devoted to preserving the rites of these gods through secret rituals, many involving devotion to the ancient Hekate.

Hekate appears in many forms: as a singular character or as a triple-faced collection of women, sometimes with the heads of animals. She was sometimes associated with bulls and described as bull-headed or bull-faced.[5] When depicted as three identical goddesses, the figures commonly ranged around a pillar either staring out, or standing archaically stiff amid the folds of their robes, or striding in a circle; and were distinguished by the articles they held: the torch, libation bowl, and fruit, with dogs at their feet.[6] She appears on earth in sacred spaces, or where three roads met, her head crowned in oak, coils of serpents around her shoulders.[7]

It was said that when she was summoned, one could not look upon her because they would be destroyed, for she was too "terrible" to look upon. She must do her work unobserved, as seeing her would send her back to the underworld, preventing her from completing her task, which could have led to disastrous consequences for the person who interrupted her.[8] Sometimes called the far-seeing lady brandishing fire,

Hekate was also called "Artemis of the gates," who could rush among the noise of the chase, a terrible sight for men to behold or hear, unless one had been through her rites of initiation and purification.[9]

Her name may have the same root as Hekatos, a masculine version meaning "worker from afar."[10] The name may also come from *ekato*, meaning "hundred."[11] This number may have indicated her connection with hecatombs, places of ritual sacrifice where the traditional offering was one hundred oxen, or because she was supposed to possess the power of compelling the ghosts of the unburied, who were doomed to walk the earth for a hundred years.[12] Alternatively, members of the Pythagorean cult, who believed that numerical harmony was the basis of the entire universe, honored ten as the most perfect number. Ten times ten being one hundred, and this number being potentially connected to Hekate, may suggest that she was considered a goddess of great harmony and perfection. She was often called Hekate Triformis, Triceps, or Trimorphis, titles which honored her three-formed identity. For this reason, mullet fish were sacrificed to her because they bred three times in a year.[13]

It was believed that Hekate could bestow the power of prophecy on mortals and facilitate communication between humankind and the divine. Therefore, Hekate was also invoked at oracular shrines. She was thought to control the elements, landscape, moon, and stars, and was displayed alongside other deities and worshipped at city gates and at entranceways to temples of other gods.

Images of Hekate often show three identical women, usually holding three different objects. Those objects would usually include a torch, a set of keys, or plants such as poppy or grain. In Roman-era temples, she was often seen with a torch, a dog, a whip, and a key, or a combination of these items. She was associated with ghosts or nightmares. Some evidence suggests that in later centuries, when Christianity was being established as a serious competitor for allegiance in the imperial world, Hekate was seen as a representative of Pagan cults and a main rival in promoting the new religion.[14]

In a literal sense, Hekate was the guardian of places where three roads met. In a symbolic sense, she helped souls navigate crossroads between the world of the living and the underworld inhabited by the dead. Without Hekate's help, the soul of a deceased person might wander between the worlds for eternity, never finding rest. Hekate was considered a queen of such lost souls. Later interpretations said she ensouled the cosmos and the people within it, and formed the connective boundary between the human and divine worlds—celestial and potentially beneficial, rather than chthonic (underworldly) and threatening.[15]

Hekate was also a goddess of fertility. She is sometimes described as a maiden or a virgin, but it might be more appropriate to describe her as unmarried. In the myths, Hekate has no spouse but she is also a mother, implying that she took male lovers on occasion.

A goddess of victory and success, she was believed to support farmers, travelers, and soldiers. She was also a guardian of newborns and was revered as a great cosmic life-force, sought by those who wished to overcome vice and attain virtue. She was believed to sit beside those dispensing judgment. She cared for the young and embodied the light of the dawn. Lastly, she guided souls through the realms of death, and in some interpretations back into life in a new incarnation.

At the same time, Hekate was connected with darkness and dread, and the most terrifying mystery of all: death. She was said to dwell in tombs or near the blood of murdered persons. She was sometimes known as Brimo, a frightening goddess attended by ghosts.[16] She was thought to send forth demons and spirits from the underworld at night. But Hekate was also thought to linger at the crossroads in order to teach sorcery and Witchcraft to those who sought her.

Then, as now, Hekate was a goddess of magick and a patroness to sorcerers and Witches. The magick she wrought took many forms: the power to heal or to kill, to punish and to find justice, to protect the traveler and the home, or to curse another. She was frequently associated with the mysterious and frightening elements of life, such as ghosts, nightmares, and the unknowable afterlife. But as much as she drew fear, Hekate also attracted fervent devotion from her followers.

But whether history assigned her the cosmos or the cold realms of the underworld, she was a goddess of and to Witches. Medea, a Witch and central character of a key Greek tragedy, summoned Hekate repeatedly in her stories.

We also see glimpses of Hekate's history as a goddess for Witches when we look at some Greek poetry. Theocritus (300–260 BCE) wrote several pieces describing the everyday life of his contemporaries. In one such piece, he wrote about a young woman named Simaetha, who cast a spell on a young athlete. After speaking to professional spellcasters, she gathered barley groats, bay leaves, bran, wax, wine, milk, and water. She also gathered an herb called coltsfoot and a pulverized lizard. Using a magick wheel, a bull-roarer, and a bronze gong, she shredded a fringe from her lover's cloak and threw it into the flames.[17] She then used various incantations to the full moon and to Hekate in the underworld, presumably believing that Hekate was present both above and below her.

HEKATE'S HISTORY

Although Hekate plays a vital role in some well-known Greek myths, she is a central character in but a few of these stories, so it is not always clear how influential she was as a whole. In addition, Hekate was worshipped in many different places and by many diverse cultures.

Her diverse veneration is believed to predate ancient Greece; thus, connecting with a single historical and cultural context is difficult.

Most of what we know about Hekate comes from descriptions of rituals and devotions dedicated to her, particularly those in ancient Greece and Rome—but these give us only a taste of who she was to the people of antiquity. Hekate may have been a household deity honored both in temples and in homes, perhaps so ubiquitous that she needed no myths to explain her. Likewise, the practice and nature of Hekate veneration varied widely depending on the region. Both the Greeks and Romans were traveled peoples. Their own gods may have collected traits from these foreign deities. Hekate may have been absorbed into Greek and Roman culture by well-traveled citizens or brought to them by immigrants from neighboring countries. Others argue that Hekate was not originally an Olympian god but rather one who belonged to a popular folk religion.[18] Whatever the truth may be, Hekate's diverse and sometimes contradictory form endured through millennia. Today, Hekate is commonly thought of as a moon goddess with a threefold identity as a young maiden, a middle-aged mother, and an elderly crone. This description is more recent and a product of contemporary neo-Pagan beliefs.

Hekate's evolution had three stages:

Phase one: an eastern "great goddess" of solar rather than lunar attributes.

Phase two: a preeminent goddess of ghosts, magick, and the moon.

Phase three: a terrifying goddess, but also one with an emphasis on a cosmic life-force with soul-nurturing virtues.[19]

Hekate is often called an ancient goddess, but it might be more accurate to say she is a modern goddess with ancient roots. Modern Hekate worship tends to be most influenced by the second and third phases listed above. Hekate particularly draws devotion from those who practice magickal arts—including and especially those who self-identify as Witches.

BEING A WITCH TODAY

Like Hekate, the Witch has enjoyed many shifts and evolution over the centuries. Historically and sometimes even today, the word Witch has been a derogatory term, eliciting images of wicked women mixing herbs and making potions with the intent to poison or curse someone. As ecofeminism grew, it encompassed feminine empowerment and love for the earth, evoking images of healers and revolutionaries. When I first came into Witchcraft in the early 2000s, Witchcraft often suggested a return to the old religions of one's own ancestry. Today, a Witch can be a person of any gender, and its classification is broadly defined. As more people become less trustful of the religions of their childhood, they are feeding their souls with herbs and chants, and looking for guidance in the rain, moon, sun, and tides.

Witchcraft has existed in the corners of every society. A Witch could have been the grandmother who could cure a chest cold by waving a rosary over it, or the old blind man at the end of the lane who told a person's fortune by tracing his finger on their palm. The individuals in these examples might not have called themselves Witches, but their power was feared and revered nonetheless. Even in this age of technology, science, and fundamental religions that often denounce such things, storefront psychics flourish and Witchcraft stores are easy to find. The Witch isn't "back"; the Witch never went anywhere. But the Witch has become a prominent fixture and, as in past years, remains connected to Hekate.

For me, I appreciate the label of Witch being attached to feminism, art, and activism, but I personally define a Witch as someone who works with magick; that is, using spells, rituals, and connection with spirit to create change. This is the sort of Witch with whom Hekate has historically shared a connection. There is little about Hekate that is *not* about the Witch. Indeed, I couldn't separate her from the Witch any more than I could separate her from the crossroads, the keys, the stars, or the graveyard.

Do I believe that one needs to identify as a Witch to honor Hekate? Certainly not. But just as non-Witches may occasionally enjoy having a Witch as a friend (you never know when you're going to need someone to chase a nasty ghost out of your house!), having a goddess of Witches on your side can be beneficial.

At the same time, like Witchcraft, Hekate can feel destructive. Many who begin the path of Witchcraft turn around quickly when spells backfire. Likewise, those who seek Hekate (or any deity, really) often find chaos injected into their lives. When the gods enter our lives, they move things around. But the consequences and chaos are often tough blessings—hurtful or restrictive elements we've become accustomed to get whisked away, and in time beautiful things replace them. These transitions can be rough, but they are the lifeblood of Hekate. As goddess of the crossroads, she guides souls through liminal spaces, both actual and symbolic.

As a Witch, hiding from Hekate is like trying to hide from the moon. We can hide in our home, but the light will eventually find its way through our window. One of the first mysteries of Hekate is to face our own pain and the shadow, to hug it and love it hard. And then, we must prepare for change. We cannot look at the moon one night and expect that it will be the same the following night. When we bring Hekate into our lives, we must know that, like the moon, she will change the plans we had for ourselves.

I had a plan for this book. I lined up the chapters in a way that mirrored my other books, giving the reader the opportunity to examine each aspect of the goddess through the context of the original culture that worshipped her, while connecting them with modern practices. But the more I tried to stick with that comfortable formula, the more elusive this book became. At last, I surrendered to the reality that this book would be different. One, Hekate's origins are too vast and span too many centuries to adequately look at these different parts of her individually. Two, it is difficult to separate the key keeper from the guardian of the crossroads, or the queen of the underworld from the queen of the cosmos. Within each of these sections, pieces of them overlap.

Lastly, I feel that Hekate simply wanted something different.

With so many people now identifying as Witches, this book needed to be more than just Hekate's myths and personal practices. While you will find those things within these pages, you'll also find an exploration of what it means to be a Witch, using Hekate as a model and a guide. While there are no rules about who can be a Witch, there are certain experiences that will prove to strengthen the understanding of being a Witch and therefore strengthen the magick.

USING THIS BOOK

Like Hekate, this book is a bridge between the old and the new. It explores the old myths while offering contemporary reflections on them. It is meant for both the novice and the seasoned practitioner. I urge you to come to this work with an open heart and mind. This work is personal and explorative. Take your time with it and see what it has for you. What I offer about Hekate and magick might not always resonate with you. I strongly advise keeping a journal as you explore the topics in this book, writing down thoughts and observations.

Each chapter includes a ritual or practice designed to help you get to know the goddess better. If you've been called to this book, Hekate is already reaching out to you. She will reveal herself in a personal way, but the hope here is for the book to provide context. The magickal workings include supplies that are generally easy to obtain, but unless otherwise noted, feel free to exchange the ingredients with what you have in your own stash of magickal treasures.

The chapters also include a mix of personal stories from modern Hekate devotees as well as ancient references to Hekate. This is intentional and is meant to show how many aspects of Hekate have grown and changed, but also how many remain as they were several thousand years ago. Just as my own stories and reflections are meant to inspire but not prescribe, so too are these stories. Let them affirm and excite you, but know your own experience with Hekate will be unique to you.

Hekate is vast and infinite, like the very universe she represents. She is the key holder, the torchbearer. She brings light into dark. She brings shape to the void. All of who she is could not be fully detailed in a whole library, let alone a single book, so remember that this work is only a piece of who she is—but because you have picked it up, she is calling to you to know more.

Let us begin.

CONNECTING WITH A GODDESS

One of the questions I often hear from new Witches or a would-be devotee of a specific goddess is, How does one know if a deity has called them?

The good news: you get to decide for yourself if Hekate is calling you.

The bad news: you get to decide for yourself if Hekate is calling you.

In some traditions, such as those of African traditional religions, specific rituals or divinations are required by an initiated priest or priestess of that tradition to determine if the deity and path are right for the seeker. While Greek Paganism and Hekatean practices remain a living tradition, most modern practitioners will need to confirm their Hekate calling on their own. The freedom in this is that a person can follow their own leanings and decide for themselves if a deity is calling to them. A restriction is that it leaves lots of room for self-doubt. It's human nature to crave structure, or at least answers. Some traditions of contemporary Witchcraft have initiated priests or priestesses of a deity who can help you determine if that deity is indeed trying to get your attention; but even so, someone curious about Hekate will ultimately need to determine this for themselves.

I believe that if you have picked up this book, Hekate has something she wants to share with you. Does she want to be your only goddess? Does she want your full devotion in this lifetime? Is she appearing only for a short but insightful adventure? I can't tell you those things—no one can. But what I can offer are some techniques, exercises, and stories that may help you make sense of your experiences with Hekate, or bring a little more of her into the magick you make.

Many Witches keep an altar of Hekate, or other deity, in their home. Ideally, this space is dedicated solely to a deity and is tended regularly with offerings. Leaving offerings for a god or goddess is an ancient practice. In doing so, an image or statue is effectively treated like a human being; in the classical period of ancient Greece (500–400 BCE), monthly food offerings were set out before statuettes of Hekate because the goddess needed to eat.[20] In leaving offerings for the goddess, you are communicating to the deity that you are, one, opening a way for a relationship with her; and two, designating a specific place where you will connect. If you cannot keep an altar in your home, a nearby park is a lovely place to meet the goddess. (Be safe.)

Many modern Witches like to give the goddess a taste of one of her native homelands and might include olives, dates, or stuffed fig leaves. Wine is also a popular offering. However, anything that is beautiful or delicious is acceptable: coffee, tea, candies, fruit, flowers. Given that Hekate was an underworld deity, foods that grow beneath the soil are particularly appropriate, such as garlic or onions. The ancient Greeks sacrificed animals to her, lamb being a favorite, but they also left her part of their regular meals.

When making offerings, don't exceed your own boundaries. For example, if you are working to maintain sobriety, offer juice instead of alcohol. If you are allergic to foods that the goddess is often offered, offer something else instead. Imagine a good friend or a neighbor is coming by. What might you offer them? Maybe a cup of coffee and a cookie? That makes for a fine offering for deities, too!

If you make your offering outdoors, don't include foods that might sicken an animal. Never underestimate the value of singing a song, reciting a poem, or painting a picture. If your sacred spot is outdoors, a regular practice of collecting trash is a marvelous offering.

Making offerings regularly will open a relationship with a goddess. I recommend including this practice as part of a routine before you ask for help from a god or goddess or invite them into your spellwork. Just as you'd want to establish a friendship with a person (have lunch with them, maybe buy them a coffee once in a while) before asking for a favor, it's simply polite!

THREE RITUALS TO KNOW HEKATE

There is no single way to honor any goddess. Introducing yourself to a goddess is best done with personal inspiration, but if you'd like some help in devising that introduction, I've included three different ways to better know Hekate. Make accommodations as necessary for yourself. These rituals are not prescriptions—they are made to be edited and improvised. Remember, magick is a creative process and thrives with personal touch. Be sure to leave your own touch on any working you do.

Some traditional times to contact Hekate include the new moon or the thirtieth day of the month. Religious calendars found at Ephesus (an ancient Greek city on the coast of what is now Turkey) say that sacrifices were made to Hekate on the first, second, and seventh days of the month, and so those dates are other options.[21] In magick, there are lots of best practices but few absolutes. If you can commit to honoring Hekate on one of her traditional days, great! Tradition does lend strength to magickal practice. But if you can't, it's better to connect with Hekate, or any deity, whenever you are able rather than not connect with them at all.

I have found that routine practice, no matter the routine, lends strength to magick—especially in the beginning of a relationship with a deity. Carving out ten minutes a night for the first month you work with Hekate to light a candle or offer a prayer will open greater connection with her than doing a highly elaborate but sporadic ritual. It's like dating someone new: initially, you may want to spend lots of time with each other to best get to know one another; but once the relationship has been established, you may not need as much time together to maintain a connection. The same will be true with the deities you work with.

A Ritual at Home

Many metaphysical stores carry statues of Hekate, but if you cannot or do not want to buy one, printing an image from the internet will be fine as well. Artistic people may want to draw a picture of her, which is a wonderful gift to the goddess. Whether you buy, print, or create your image of Hekate, you can also include images or figurines of the animals that are sacred to Hekate, such as the owl, the dog, the bear, or the deer.

Greek gods are thought to be fond of wine, but if you do not have or do not want to use wine, using juice, tea, milk, or a glass of your favorite soda is equally delightful. The gods appreciate authenticity. Offer something that is authentic to you and they will respond in kind. I often offer the first flowers to bloom in my garden.

What you'll need:

- Three candles—black, white, and silver, or a combination
- An image of Hekate
- A bulb of garlic
- A libation

If you keep an altar, set these things on it. You do not have to keep the altar set up around the clock, but it's beneficial for your magick and your relationship with Hekate if you can keep it up most of the time.

Wherever you have set your space, light the candles and offer this prayer:

> Lady of the crossroads, the key keeper, the moon lady,
> I seek to know you, I seek to hear you.
> I am here, I am here, I am here.
> Hekate Triformus, be with me now.

Sit in silence for a few minutes. If thoughts pop up, let them drift away. Sometimes, people expect a specific experience, thinking the goddess's words must be loud and profound. This can happen, but more often the work is quiet and the gods' voices are muted. Ultimately, they will come through dreams, moments of synchronicity, or a personal revelation or understanding.

When I first performed this rite, I didn't feel anything aside from a sense of peace and a surprising feeling of familiarity. However, the next day I went to the library to research Hekate, and I got a phone call from an old friend whom I hadn't spoken to in years. She was at a crossroads in her relationship, and she needed a place to stay.

By opening our home to our friend, my husband and I, like Hekate, became keepers of the crossroads while our friend figured out which path to walk.

A Ritual Outside

Hekate was historically honored through preparing meals and leaving them at crossroads, perhaps with the intention that a hungry person would find them. Leaving a food offering at a crossroads (such as at a T intersection) or any place a hungry person might find it is one way to do this rite. When I was living in New York, I often felt that the subway was a place of Hekate, given that it was literally underground, and I often made Hekate devotions there. Today, I leave meals at an intersection close to where people without housing often camp.

When preparing the food, say this prayer:

> Lady of the crossroads, the key keeper, the moon lady,
> I seek to know you, I seek to hear you.
> I am here, I am here, I am here.
> Hekate Triformus, help me to help.

A Ritual in the Community

Hekate is fond of animals, particularly dogs. There are few greater ways to please a deity than to care for the animals they love. Consider volunteering at an animal shelter, or even giving your favorite four-legged creature an extra yummy treat.

As you begin your work, speak your intention to the goddess. A suggested incantation is: "Through the will of your work, thus I open the door to knowing you."

FORMING THE RELATIONSHIP

Just as forming a relationship with a person takes time, exploration, and trust, so does forming a relationship with a divine being. Hekate will have her own way of doing things, and you may find that she wants to rearrange things in your life. One woman I know was quite settled in her home, but a series of events occurring shortly after her dedication to Hekate found her moving a thousand miles west, where a grand purpose and great adventure awaited her. Another lost a relationship quite suddenly, but she met the true love of her life almost immediately after. Your story will be unique. You could very well experience similar upheaval. Alternatively, you may find that a deep sense of peace comes into your life. When I formally invited Hekate into my home, I found myself having to face old ghosts and parts of myself that I had previously avoided. People I hadn't spoken to in years returned. Some of these encounters were quite uncomfortable, others were joyful, but all were blessed.

Your own experience will be blessed, too. Open yourself to that blessing, no matter the form it takes!

CHAPTER TWO

The Witch in the Family

*Hekate, I believe, is not meant to be explained or be completely
transparent like some deities. I believe her essence is unexplainable:
a feeling, a gesture, the mystery of the Magick. How you choose the
materials for the spells and rituals, communing with the spirits and your
ancestors . . . all these acts are in her name. That, my friend, is when you
are tapping into your inner Witch. Perhaps that is why the archetype
of the Witch has never really faded. There has been one in every
culture. The Italians call them Strega, the Yoruba call them Aje. Where
my mother is from, they call them* brujas, brujos, santigueras, *and*
curanderos. *Here, we call them Witch. In Espiritismo, there is mention
of a spirit guide known as La Brujita ("the little witch"), which there is
very little information on, yet everyone has one. For me, I feel there is a
link between Espiritismo, Hekate, and the archetype of the Witch.*

—WILSON JOEL RIOS, MODERN DEVOTEE OF HEKATE

Our families define us, whether we like it or not. Hekate's family is no exception. Her patronage includes the stars and the underworld, the moon and the earth, along with a host of other gods who are sometimes her parents, her children, or her siblings. Like many people, her family and history are complicated.

Most of what we know of her comes from poetic devotional prayers, which could reflect a consensus of who she was to those who worshipped her, or merely an individual author's personal vision of her. Just as murky and mysterious as the cosmos she ruled, Hekate's "true" ancient identity is unknowable. But just as a star may appear brighter when a gazer looks at one nearby rather than directly at it, it may help to better understand Hekate by looking at the myths of those close to her.

THE ANCIENTS AND THEIR GODS

While Hekate existed before the ancient Greeks, it is their influence and interpretation of the goddess most modern Witches know, so that will be the focus of this section. It may be helpful to remember that these myths were collected from a wide geographic region in a time when most people (aside from voyagers or soldiers) rarely traveled. One community's idea of a goddess might be very different from those of people even fifty miles away. It may also be helpful to remember that these myths were cultivated over several thousand years. Time and variety among cultures may have twisted and gnarled Hekate's family tree. It may be tempting to adhere to one and ignore the others, perhaps to soothe a logical mind, but doing so undermines the beautiful complexity of these great tales. It's fine to pick a favorite, but let us never ignore the others, even when they confuse us or make us uncomfortable.

Gods are, and have always been, reflections of human experience. Most modern mainstream religions have a central god figure who is the epitome of perfection, which perhaps reflects a contemporary belief that perfection is even possible and lives are meant to achieve that. This has not always been the case in every religion or era. The ancient Greeks may have believed that perfection was possible, but their gods were not all-knowing and always right. These deities were more like exaggerated versions of mortals. Their deeds were greater, their accomplishments more heroic. Their romances were more passionate and more devastating. Their virtues were deeper and their physique more beautiful, but their flaws were greater. They could be magnanimous, but also terrible. These deities, as well as pre-Christian gods and their mythologies, often served as the great lessons of humanity, tactile examples of what to do or what to avoid. Ancient peoples prayed to these gods, but in many cases the rites and rituals existed as much to appease the gods as to distract them from interfering with people's daily lives.

Among the Olympian gods, Hekate was considered older and wiser than most. Yet, because her mythology offers fewer stories, we don't have as many examples of her being as flawed as Zeus, as vengeful as Hera, or as jealous as Aphrodite. However, we do know that she challenged others, engaged in battle, picked sides, and helped take her chosen side to victory, but whether her choice was selected because of its strength or righteousness we cannot know.

Many members of Hekate's family are introduced via the story of Zeus overthrowing the Titans. Titans were godlike beings who embodied the greatest forces of nature—the sea, the sky, the earth. Prior to this overthrow, two of the Titans, Uranus (Sky) and Gaia (Earth), fell in love and had many children together. One of their sons, Kronus (sometimes spelled Cronus, who represented the destructive force of time), feared the power of his own children and swallowed them at birth. To protect the life of their one remaining son, Kronus's sister and wife, Rhea, swaddled a rock and gave it to him. Thinking it was his infant son, Kronus swallowed the rock and Rhea raised their child, Zeus, in secret. Zeus later overthrew the Titans and became king of the gods. In many interpretations, Hekate was an aunt of Zeus, and although she was considered a

Titan herself, she helped her nephew to victory. She also assisted the gods in their war with the Gigantes, a savage race of humans who were chased away because of their insolence toward the gods, and slew a giant named Clytius.[1] In other stories, Hekate was a daughter of Zeus.

According to the Greek writer Hesiod, Hekate was loved, or at least respected, by Zeus. While she was certainly honored by the Olympian gods, Hekate did not live with them on the great mountain of Olympus. Instead, she preferred a cave, far from Olympus. Her far-off abode has been illustrated by some translations of her name: "far-off" or "far-darting." These titles might also represent attributes she possessed, which were both awful and mysterious.[2] True to her legacy of victory, areas of her patronage included victory in battle and success in sports, as well as aiding horsemen, sailors, fishermen, farmers, and shepherds; ensuring successful reproduction of livestock; and caring for newborns.

Hekate's realms also included places considered dark and scary by ancient peoples—the darkest depths of the sea, where great monsters supposedly swam, where sailors who ventured beyond the horizon might not return. It's possible that Zeus gave Hekate a rather backhanded gift: an area of the world that the other gods abhorred or feared. Alternately, because of her age and wisdom, she may have had greater understanding of these mysterious places. Zeus may have recognized that Hekate was the only deity fit to reign over these frightful areas. Or perhaps even Zeus, king of the gods, feared his aunt, and wanted to keep in her good graces by giving her a gift he thought she might like.

OTHER FAMILY MEMBERS

Hekate's Great-Grandparents

Hekate's great-grandmother was Gaia, whose body was the great quiet earth, existing long before humans walked on it. Because her body was the actual earth, Gaia held the realm of the dead. Calling upon the dead for insight into the present and prophecies for the future was a common practice in the Old World, and so Gaia and therefore Hekate were oracular goddesses who could deliver messages or warnings about the future to the mortal world.[3] Hekate's great-grandfather was Uranus, whose name referred to the heavens, or the great expanse of sky. Hekate was also equated with the Platonic cosmic soul, which may have come through her ancestral lineage of sky and earth.[4]

Hekate's Grandparents

Uranus and Gaia were the parents of Phoebe. Phoebe was Hekate's maternal grandmother, who was also associated with prophecy and the oracles. Hekate's maternal grandfather was the benevolent god Coesus, also known as the axis of the world,[5] and associated with oracles and prophecy.[6] Coesus is sometimes a brother of Zeus, who helped castrate Uranus.

Hekate's paternal grandfather was Crius, a brother of Coesus, who was linked to the ram and the constellation of Aries. Hekate was also sometimes said to be the granddaughter of Helios, who was the personification of the sun and an all-seeing force.[7] Later, Hekate would corner Helios for information on finding Persephone. Her paternal grandmother was Eurybia, who had mastery over the sea and all natural forces of wind and constellations.[8]

Hekate's Parents

Hekate was said to be the daughter of Asteria and Perses. In other renditions, Zeus and Asteria were her parents. In still other tellings, Hekate was said to be the only child and a direct descendant of Gaia, Ouronos, and Okeanos (Earth, Sky, and Sea).[9] In a more brutal description of Hekate, the goddess was described as a bloodthirsty daughter of a king named Perses, who went on to bear Circe and Medea to her uncle Aeetes, king of Colchis.[10] In yet another description, she was referred to simply as "child of the night."[11]

Hekate's mother, Asteria (who was also said to be associated with Brizo, meaning slumber), was associated with divination by dreams, the starry sky, falling stars, and possibly astrology. She too was likely an oracular goddess particularly associated with dream oracles, who may have been worshipped on Delos, an island between Greece and Turkey. While a barren island, it was also an important religious site. In antiquity, women visited this place to seek news about their seafaring husbands or sons. In another myth, Asteria gives shelter to Leto, who, pregnant with Artemis and Apollo, could find no place to give birth, as Zeus's jealous wife Hera had placed a curse on her. Via her mother's influence, Hekate gained the powers of oracular visions, as well as being a protector of women in childbirth.

In other accounts, Hekate is the daughter of Demeter, the grain mother. This equates Hekate with Persephone, who was both the youthful maiden of springtime and the queen of the cold underworld of death.[12] In Demeter's most famous myth, Hekate acts as an aunt or godmother by helping Demeter find Persephone and by being a surrogate mother to Persephone. Other mothers of Hekate include Cynthia (a moon goddess), Ortygia (associated with the quail), Chlamydia (meaning cloak), Cynethus (associated with the dog), and Pyripile (meaning fiery). One Thessalian story says that Hekate was the daughter of Pheraen, a newborn infant thrown out onto the crossroads who was rescued and brought up by shepherds.[13]

We don't know what kind of child Hekate was, but we can gather by at least one story that she wasn't particularly dutiful. In one myth in which Zeus is her father, Hekate enrages her mother Hera by stealing her rouge and giving it to Europa, one of her father's mistresses. Hekate then fled to earth and hid in the house of a woman in labor. In one story in which she is the daughter of Perses, she tests poisons on strangers in the temple of Artemis.[14]

HEKATE: THE SPOUSELESS

Hekate was not known to have married or coupled with any specific god, and she is often described as a maiden or virgin. The title of virgin in this context does not mean Hekate never experienced sex, but rather that she was unmarried. In some cases, Hekate was said to have offspring with some men.[15] Although not without partners or lovers, she was not specifically known for having a single, devoted person of her own.

HEKATE'S CHILDREN

Prior to her adoption by the Greeks, Hekate is believed to have been an all-purpose mother goddess. As she was adopted deeper into the Greek traditions, she began to take on relatives and siblings.

Hekate was sometimes said to be the mother of Skylla, who had the torso and head of a female but multiple legs, which were sometimes part canine and part fish. Skylla was associated with Sicily and the Strait of Messina, a treacherous body of water, as well as the magickal arts, wisdom, wise counsel, and prudence.[16] She shared some similarities with the mermaid and could drag sailors to their deaths, representing the rocky shores that could devastate ships before they were ever noticed.

ONE AND THE SAME WITH OTHER GODDESSES?

Hekate is sometimes synonymous with Artemis, goddess of the moon. The two may have represented different phases of the moon. Both Hekate and Artemis were honored in a full moon festival in April or May, suggesting that they were honored conjointly as two different aspects of the same goddess.[17] Other interpretations suggest that they are the same goddess but at different points of life, Artemis being the young maiden and Hekate the elderly, wizened crone. It may even be that these two goddesses were aspects of one singular goddess from an earlier era. Because the moon was frequently connected to reproduction, both Artemis and Hekate were believed to protect women in childbirth.

If Hekate and Artemis are one and the same, then the sun god Apollo could be said to be Hekate's brother, who was often said to be Artemis's twin brother. Both Hekate and Apollo were credited with delivering divine messages, and they shared the description "far-off" or "far-darting."[18]

As mentioned above, Hekate was sometimes equated with Persephone, and other times with Demeter.[19] Hekate, the most ancient goddess of the underworld, becomes, along with Persephone, the "divinity par excellence" of Witches.[20] Persephone is sometimes connected with the triune of Hekate, Artemis, and Selene, the lunar goddess who presides over nocturnal rites. Selene was said to rule in heaven, while Artemis embodied the moonlight upon earth. Hekate represented the dark and mysterious side of the moon. Both Selene and Hekate are described as three-faced, which may also reference the moon's cycles of waxing, full, and waning. Hekate was also described as "you who with the triple forms of triple graces dance, reveling with the stars."[21]

Brimo, a goddess who sometimes formed a trio with Demeter and Persephone, was sometimes interchanged with Hekate. The name Brimo could be translated as "terrifying" and was also associated with the Roman goddess Bona Dea, who was associated with snakes and healing.[22] Hekate was also associated with a Lydian dog goddess of the underworld whose mystical patronage included bloody sacrifice, justice, and creatures of revenge.[23] Finally, Hekate and the sea god Poseidon may have shared a temple at Eleusis in the fifth century CE or before, and may have themselves been connected in some traditions.[24]

In other stories, the terrifying mythological creature of the Gorgon, a female with snakes for hair, who could turn a man to stone by looking at him, is also said to be the face of Hekate. The Greeks believed the Gorgon maintained spiritual boundaries between the different realms of existence, something Hekate (as key keeper and guardian of the crossroads) was also said to have done.[25] Both Hekate and the Gorgon were described as triple goddesses who dwelled in caves, the womb of the earth, but could command the great realms of sky, earth, underworld, and sea.

Finally, Hekate was sometimes associated with Baubo, a comical figure with breasts that double as staring eyes, whose genitals form a bearded mouth. When Demeter grieved for her missing daughter Persephone, some retellings have Baubo exposing herself, encouraging the bereft mother to laugh. This sudden exposure of hidden female genitalia shocked Demeter out of her grief, which helped fertility return to the earth. Considered both sacred and abominable, Baubo was equated with ribald humor. Her name conjures the "baying" of a hound, another trait identifying her with Hekate.[26]

HEKATE AND HER ANIMALS

Hekate was strongly associated with several different animals. The stereotype of the Witch with a black cat, or even an owl or bat, is a common archetype, as many cultures believed that Witches could control or enter the minds of animals, or travel with animal companions by their side. Hekate not only appears with several different animals, in several poems and depictions she also has animal heads or bodies. Some of her more sacred animals were sacrificed to her.

The following list includes animals frequently considered sacred to Hekate.

Black Lamb

Lambs were common in ancient Greece and were frequently sacrificed to Hekate. Black animals in particular were thought to be sacred to her, for their assumed connection to the darkness of the underworld. In Ovid's *Metamorphoses*, Medea, who was a priestess of Hekate, sacrifices two black lambs to bring her husband's father back to life.

Bull

In some prayers, Hekate was described as having horns, a bull head, or a bull-shaped body. The reason for this is not clear, but the horned animals may suggest powers of fertility.

Dog

Dogs, especially black dogs, are perhaps Hekate's best-known animal symbol. She was said to appear on earth accompanied by hounds, whose whining and howling announced her approach. Hekate was also known as a ruler of demons that appeared in canine form.[27] An image from a fifth century BCE lekythos depicts Hekate as a dog eating the dead in Hades, which could highlight an action believed to be a necessary task delivered by a goddess of both life and death, which go hand in hand.

Dragon

Hekate sometimes appears with the head of a dragon, but depending on the translation this may have meant water serpent, which may highlight her connection to both the depths of the ocean as well as the underworld, given that serpents were frequently connected with the underworld.

Goat

As horned animals in general were associated with Hekate, the goat may be among them. Hekate is a special patroness among shepherds. In some rituals, goats may have been sacrificed to her. This too may be a symbol for fertility.

Horse

The horse is another guise of Hekate, when she appears with different animal heads. Like the association with the goat, the horse may reflect Hekate's periodic patronage of shepherds. The horse may also represent a kind of soul fire, which is explored in the *Chaldean Oracles*, a set of spiritual texts in which Hekate is prominently featured.[28] The horse may also have represented a demon spirit that served Hekate.[29]

Lion

Images of Hekate routinely include lions sitting by her side, which may indicate a Middle Eastern origin, where they were a common feature. The appearance of these animals may also suggest a dominion over land, as well as sea and sky. Hekate references lions in the

Chaldean Oracles, suggesting that things will appear "in lion form" to those who summon her regularly.

Owl

One of many creatures connected with Hekate is the owl, a bird who can see through darkness, just as the torchbearer herself might. The owl also silently swoops down to devour live prey and is therefore directly associated with death. Burial urns in the form of owls have been discovered, dating back to 300 BCE. The Near East, Western Anatolia, the Aegean, and Central Europe associate the owl with regeneration. As a symbol of prophecy and wisdom, the owl became another animal of Hekate.[30] Because of her connection to the owl, she may also have a distant association with Athena, who is also frequently associated with the owl.

Serpent

Hekate has been shown wearing crowns of serpents, carrying them, and holding them about her waist. The snake image represents Hekate's powers of the underworld. Sacred serpents are the mark of a chthonian spirit, *chthonian* meaning a presence from the underworld.[31] Being an animal that burrows under the ground, the serpent was often connected with deities who had power over the dead. The image of Hekate holding the snakes may also suggest a protective nature.

• • •

Hekate is also associated with the cat, the cow, the frog, the pig, the sheep, and the wolf. Exploring her relationship to all of these creatures is beyond the scope of this book. However, it is important to note their general connection to Hekate, as during your journeys with her, she may appear in such forms—either in dreams or meditations, or through synchronistic appearances by living animals.

THE WITCH IN THE FAMILY

In the war against the Titans, Hekate fought under the agreement that she could maintain her role among the gods as a patroness of the earth, sky, and sea. Out of either respect or fear, Zeus agreed to this arrangement and left her alone to do her work. Hekate did not sit among the gods on Mount Olympus, preferring to "sit afar" from the rest. Because of her age and diverse origins, Hekate served as a bridge from an old regime to a new one, as well as one connecting different cultures and eras. But if today's mainstream religions are considered "the new," Hekate now serves as a bridge to the old. This is not going backward, but rather putting new life into an older practice. As more people find themselves identifying with alternative spiritualities, Hekate serves as a bridge to the future. This forward-focused role is as ancient to Hekate as the myths are to us.

Through a different lens, Hekate comes from fractured patronage, a family in turmoil. She rebels against authority; she lives alone, away from the rest of her family. She inherited powerful gifts from her ancestors, and gives birth to things that terrify others. Some of her relatives fear her, while others respect her. A great number seem to pretend that she doesn't exist at all.

Hekate is the stereotypical Witch in the family.

If Hekate were cast in a cliché movie role, she might be the weird aunt whose past is something of a family secret, but who regales the littlest ones with fascinating tales of faeries and sprites. She may also be the elusive cousin who blocks all the family on social media, secretly reading Tarot for her cousins in the spare room at holiday gatherings. She might also be the relative who helps the rest of the family understand the choices of the misfit one, either the one who dropped out of college, or the one who quit their six-figure job to pursue a risky dream. Maybe she's the eccentric grandparent who knows the right thing to say during heartbreak, the one with the power and confidence to speak over the most cruel and critical voices at the dinner table.

Someone who identifies as a Witch may find Hekate's stories familiar. Perhaps you, like her, were the strange one in your family, the one whom others snickered at behind their back . . . but also the one that people would seek out when they had nightmares or needed help getting the "icky feeling" out of the house. Perhaps you had psychic gifts, had dreams that could come true, or experienced visits from spirits in the night. The family might have known about your gifts and even joked about them from time to time, but never questioned them. Maybe they harshly tried to deny your gifts, or even exorcise them from you. You might have been shunned for your gift. Other Witches I've met come from a line of magickal people, or their gifts are embraced and openly discussed in their families. Some say they were part of the side of the family who does "that stuff," while the other side of the family "doesn't do that stuff and goes to church," and the two sides never speak at all.

Maybe other reasons set you apart from your family. Maybe you were bookish while they were sporty, or you identified as a different gender from the one you were assigned at birth. Maybe they struggled to accept the people you love. Perhaps you, like Hekate, rebelled against the order you were born into, be that a religion, social class, political affiliation, or system of prejudice. Just as Hekate helped Zeus overthrow her own ancestors, most Witches are rebellious in one way or another. Often, the circumstances that lead us to rebel are the same ones that nudge us into Witchcraft. Maybe your story is something else altogether.

THE WITCH IN THE FAMILY

I come from a large and largely conservative family, a mix of Catholics and Southern Baptists. As a child, I was a devout Christian, but I was also obsessed with magick, fairy tales, and movies like *Bedknobs and Broomsticks*. I begged my older cousin to tell me ghost stories—not the urban legends I heard at slumber parties, but the *real* ones—the encounters she herself had, or those of someone she knew directly. I drew Ouija boards on notebook paper to contact the dead during recess and read Tarot for my Catholic high school classmates. Witchcraft comes to us at different times. Some of us figure it out young, but plenty don't embrace the title until much later in life. Finding Witchcraft knows no age. Being a Witch is not confined to a single gender, race, or religion. Witches are in every corner of every faith and culture, taking different forms and reflecting what is scary and out of reach for the dominant culture. Even within that, our Witchcraft will shape and evolve, just as the moon does, and just as Hekate has.

Also, like Hekate, many Witches find comfort in some sort of separation. Like all people, some Witches have great relationships with their families, while others do not. Some are introverted; others enjoy lots of social interaction. No matter how much they enjoy the company of others, many Witches find that they need periods of space and quiet. Magick, like the depths of the sea that Hekate governs, is immense and needs time and space. Our experiences are intense and generally will need time to process.

It's not easy being the Witch in the family. Hekate may have had good reason to stay away from Olympus. Perhaps she, like other Witches, felt misunderstood and chose solitude over ridicule or discomfort. Many of us are lucky and find communities of other Witches, but even within those communities loneliness may be present. Witches are unique, and it's possible to feel alone even

35

among like-minded others. No one is ever truly going to know the experiences we ourselves have undergone.

However, there is power in solitude. We can better hear the voice of Spirit when our heads aren't filled with the voices and presence of others. Toward the end of writing this book, my husband was away and I disconnected my social media profiles. This was prior to COVID-19, and I was unused to such strong isolation, but my dreams were more vivid, with more telling messages. Sometimes allowing ourselves this kind of space, when possible, can help us better tap into our personal power.

It is in the relationship with the ancestors that the most powerful magick can be attained. Ancestors, whether these be blood kin or beloved friends who have passed on, will be helpful allies in magickal work. Even if your living family mocks or abuses your magick, you may be surprised how quickly deceased family members will help you in your endeavors. This can be especially true if you have a staunchly agnostic or atheistic family, or a religious family who strongly shuns associations with the dead. The deceased may be starved for attention and connection with the living. The most helpful spirits for me are those of my deceased relatives—especially those who mocked me while they were living. Whenever I need protection, assistance, or something provided for me, they are spirits who immediately provide.

This does not mean that you need to form relationships with relatives who abused you, either in life or after. While death can provide the opportunity to forgive a rift or injury, no one should be expected to forgive an abusive relative. We'll discuss working with ancestors and the dead more in Chapter 5.

I am often the butt of jokes in my family for being "woo-woo" or "weird." Sometimes it's funny. Sometimes it gets old. For the most part, it's a great blessing. Being the Witch in the family is not always about casting the right spell, having the right herb, or being able to talk to ghosts in the middle of the night. Sometimes, it's bringing beauty and magick into the eyes of a child.

Two summers ago, I vacationed with my family during the Perseids meteor shower. I sat up late watching the shooting stars, and the next morning I told my little nephew about them.

"Did one fly over our house?" he asked.

"Yes," I said. "They bring sweet dreams. Did it bring you a sweet dream?"

He nodded. I promised to watch for more that night, and he asked, "If you see another one, will you tell me?" I promised I would, and I most definitely sat outside that night and waited for another. Luckily for me, I saw two. The next morning, I told my nephew that I had seen a star for both him and his sister. He said they had brought him sweet dreams again.

This was a key moment for me in understanding not just my role as the family Witch, but also Hekate's role in her own family. We often think of her in the underworld with the dead, and while that is true, she is influenced by the cosmos, too. Her realm, and her family, are both above and below. She may be the key to understanding both. For that moment with my nephew, I, like Hekate, opened the door to magick and wonder.

It's helpful to have a Witch in the family. It's helpful to be the Witch in the family. It can be a point of both pride and frustration, but it's an important role. What would Zeus have done without Hekate in his attempt to overthrow the Titans? How would Demeter have found Persephone without Hekate? There is a role in every family or community for the weird and the otherworldly. Even if this person is a source of secrecy, scorn, shame, or even anger, communities have depended on the oracular person for generations for insight into danger or otherwise. Like Hekate, the family

Witch can open the door to mystery and wonder. Magick lights the world with color, spice, and sensation. Without knowing a shooting star is flying over your house to leave you a sweet dream, it's just another bedtime.

FINDING YOURSELF IN HEKATE

Hekate's legacy is that of rebellious child, distant but caring mother, strange auntie, wise and slightly cranky older sister, coconspirator cousin. Before embracing the parts of Hekate, begin by honoring those parts within yourself.

- Whom do you care for or nurture?

- Whose power do you challenge?

- Whom do you guide?

- Whom do you boss around?

- Whom do you help, even if that means getting into a bit of trouble?

- When can you feel completely alone but still somewhat connected to the people in your life?

You may find that some of these roles overlap, just as they do in Hekate's world.

Roles change, shift, and evolve, sometimes even over the course of a day! Ask the parent who readies their children for school, shuttles them out the door, and then rushes off to a job in which they support the role of someone else, perhaps mentoring a younger colleague, before hurrying home, but not before stopping in to check on an elder. Pay attention to the roles you embody without judging or analyzing them.

Of your roles, which one feels the strongest at present? It may not be the role you embody most of the time.

Whichever one that is, invite Hekate to join you in it:

Masked Lady, Gorgon queen,
The sister, the daughter, the mother, the lover,
The cousin, the child, the one who sees,
The one who watches, the one from afar,
Stand with me in this moment,
And I will stand with you.

Light a single black or white candle. (Using either white or black is important in this instance because black is the combination of all colors and white is the absence or reflection of all color.)

Start drawing or writing using a free hand. Don't try to draw a picture that's beautiful or obsess over legibility. Let Hekate give you information about this role and how she connects it with you. Don't worry if it doesn't make a lot of sense right now. Often, when the gods come to us, they don't make a ton of sense initially. But in time the pieces come together and clarify things.

HONORING THE WITCH IN YOUR FAMILY

When being the family Witch causes you stress, it's helpful to list the things that make you unique within your family. Perhaps you're good with animals. Maybe you find the humor in situations that everyone else finds boring. Perhaps you have creative gifts unparalleled among your relatives.

Writing each of these things down is a helpful practice. You can certainly use pieces of paper, but I also recommend collecting leaves and letting them dry. Then use a marker to write down each of the things that make you unique within your family.

Next, write down the traits you've received from family members that make you strong or powerful. Just as Hekate inherited both destruction and healing, as well as the expanse of the stars above and the underworld, we inherit things from our own families. Maybe you inherited a parent's self-discipline, which is handy when remembering to do a routine devotional. Perhaps you had a grandparent who believed that ghosts walked among us, and this helped validate the experiences you had yourself. Maybe your aunt helped you develop a green thumb, and you now grow a heck of an herb garden. These familial influences need not be blood family, either. Foster family members, teachers, or family friends are absolutely valid. In many cultures, the foster family was more important than that of blood.

Collect these gifts in a jar. Decorate the jar to reflect your most beautiful Witchiness. Perhaps you want to cover the jar with images of vintage Hollywood Witches. Maybe you just want to paint the jar black. It's valid so long as it reflects you.

On the top of the jar, draw the moon, or print out a picture of the moon from the internet and attach it to the top. Consider including other symbols of Hekate, such as a key, a torch, or one of her animals. (Note: Don't seal the jar, as you may want to add things or pull things out to reread them later.)

When the jar is complete, hold it to your heart and recite the following prayer either aloud or in your mind:

Hekate, the daughter, the mother, the sister, the aunt,
Stand with me when the ground shakes,
Remind me of my feet,
Remind me of my crown.
A Witch I am,
A Witch I will be,
From the stars to the grave,
And all in between.

This is a helpful affirmation and practice for when you're feeling out of sorts about your role as the Witch within the family . . . perhaps especially before holidays!

CHAPTER THREE

Torchbearer: The Light in the Dark

O Lord Helios, O sacred flame of the torch wayfaring Hekate holds by her, which she carries as she ranges in the realm of Olympus or returns to the earth (where are) the crossroads, her sacred place, crowned with oak and woven coils of fierce serpents.
—SOPHOCLES, *RHIZOTOMOI* ("THE ROOT-CUTTERS")[1]

W hen I first started Witchcraft, someone told me that Witches should never, ever invoke Hekate. When I asked why, the person said, "I don't know. Maybe it's because she's a dark goddess?"

What does it mean to be a dark goddess, anyway?

If something is described as dark because of its association with things that many find scary, such as death, decay, pain, terror, or sorrow, then yes, Hekate is a dark goddess. Yet medical personnel, social workers, therapists, morticians, firefighters, and other civil servants work with these sorts of "dark" things too. Does that mean these are "dark" industries? Are the people who work in them scary by default? My husband is a wound care nurse, and although many people find his work unnerving, he is a warm, friendly, and caring person, as are nearly all nurses I've met. People like my husband are integral to society, a legion helping to navigate the difficult parts of life. The society that I live in does not avoid workers in these industries simply because of the nature of the work. Therefore, for me, it makes no sense to avoid Hekate because of her patronage of uncomfortable things, any more than it would make sense to avoid a surgeon because they work with blood or a mortician because they work with the dead.

At the same time, perhaps in reaction to a long period of Witchcraft being obsessed with "lightness," there has been an explosion in popularity of "dark" Witchcraft: a sort inspired by scarier things, dark clothing, hexes, or otherwise. This may also be a reaction to a general fear seizing our world at present, from ecological disaster to a global rise in fascism. We may be unconsciously drawn to that which is scary because we ourselves are scared. This certainly has its place. Witchcraft has been credited with overthrowing oppressive persons or even governments for time immemorial. Witches have always used their magick to push back against oppressors. But dark loses meaning when it becomes "dark fluff," which is a tendency to revel in things considered "dark" for their shock value or sexiness. In that case, would-be devotees might be attracted to Hekate because of her reputation of darkness, without reflecting on what that label actually means, or what a relationship with only the dark parts of a goddess might actually be. It creates a Witchcraft as shallow and meaningless as the kind of Witchcraft that focuses only on light, happy parts of life.

One lesson from Hekate, particularly in her guise of torchbearer, is that true power comes from embracing all sides, as opposed to picking and choosing points of focus because of one's personal preference. When we look closer at Hekate's role in myths and rituals, we often find her not reveling in the dark spaces she inhabits, but bringing light to them. This too may give us more insight into the role of the Witch in today's world.

HEKATE, TORCHBEARER

The flaming torch is one of Hekate's identifying traits, and one of the most long-standing. The connection with the torch was first mentioned in "Homeric Hymn to Demeter," written around 500–600 BCE. When Demeter is mourning her missing daughter Persephone and seeks help from the Olympian gods, only Hekate is willing to step up. Ten days after Persephone disappears, Hekate comes to Demeter holding "a light ablaze in her hands"—a torch.[2] Hekate confesses to Demeter that she heard Persephone cry, but she did not see where she went. Together, with Hekate's torches blazing, they begin to search for the missing girl.

Demeter was in crisis, but her situation either scared or bored her friends and relations. Hekate wasn't the only one with knowledge of where Persephone had gone. (In the next section, we learn that Helios, god of the sun, knew where the young maiden was the whole time.) It was Hekate who was willing to venture into the frightening depths of Hades to retrieve Persephone. Guided by her torches, Hekate helped another soul through the darkness.

The torch serves as one of the prime symbols for Hekate, and a main way she is identified in ancient works of art. Hekate's identity as torchbearer likely predates even her devotion in ancient Greece. Both Hekate and the moon goddess Artemis are called torchbearers, or light bearers, a title often connected with the moon.[3] Hekate's name is also often linked with fire. She is called Phosphoros, meaning "light bringer," as well as Daidoukos ("torchbearer"), Purphoros ("fire-breathing"), and Puripnon ("fire breather"), and is said to possess untiring flame in triple baskets.[4]

The torches represent Hekate's role in the underworld, but they also underscore her role in the cosmos, as the torch symbolized the moon.

THE TORCH AND THE MOON

Just as a torch brings light to a dark space, the moon brings light to a dark sky. Recalling that Zeus gave Hekate dominion of not only earth and sea but also the starry heavens, she is forever linked to the light and fire of celestial bodies—and the moon in particular. It's thought that this portrait of her as a patron of the heavens nurtured her increasing lunar identity and associations with other lunar deities such as Artemis and Selene.[5] One incantation from a Greek magickal papyrus refers to Hekate, Artemis, and Selene and references both the starry heavens as well as the flaming torches:

> . . . night-shining / triple-sounding,
>
> :
>
> Lamp-bearer, shining and aglow . . .
> Star-coursing, heav'nly, torch-breather, fire-breather, /
>
> :
>
> Give heed to me, Lady, I ask of you.[6]

In Greek culture, the moon was often imagined as a goddess and as a muse.[7] Hekate, who was associated with the moon, was called *amoibousa*: "the changing one" or "producing changes."[8] Hekate has also been described as "the oldest Venus," the manifold mother to "whom my poems go, like ladders drawn," suggesting Hekate, as embodied by the moon, was a source of creative inspiration.[9]

It is sometimes argued that Hekate was not associated with the moon until the Roman period, meaning that the moon association was a relatively late addition to Hekate's mythology. Either way, her legacy of being a goddess of the heavens helped solidify her as a patroness of the night sky, which also credited her with influence on earth. Deities and heroes linked with the moon and agricultural cycles were a sacred model for all existence; a symbol of the promise that all that dies may return to life as do buried seeds.[10] If the dark of the cave or the underworld is symbolized by the night sky, Hekate's torch may have represented the moon itself. The moon, which governed the cycles of planting for ancient peoples and inspired the very first calendars, was integral to the planning and reaping of the harvest. This source of light was therefore the guiding force for the forging of new life. The moon is also thought to sometimes symbolize Hekate's torch on the night when she and Demeter sought to find Persephone.[11]

THE TORCH AND THE SUN

Hekate and her torches are often associated with the element of fire, the light she bears derived from both moon and starlight.[12] If the moon is the sun of the night, could Hekate's torch also be a symbol of the actual sun? Hepat, a goddess of the Hurrians, is another deity linked with the origins of Hekate. The Hurrians were a Bronze-Age people who lived in roughly the same area as modern-day Armenia. Hepat may have been a goddess of the sun, whose solar attributes may have influenced Hekate's early Greek cult and might explain why Hekate is sometimes seen with solar images—her fiery nature ultimately represented by the flaming torches.[13] In this, Hekate's flaming torches also represent a powerful antiquity, and so for our modern purposes, they may represent ancestry.

THE TORCH AND RENEWAL

In her myth, Persephone followed Hekate and her lit torches to Hermes, who took her to the surface where she could be reunited with her mother, an event that would make the land fertile again. For this reason, Hekate's torches may have represented the land's fertility. Some Hekate devotees of ancient Greece carried torches around freshly sown fields to promote their fertility.[14] The torch may also have symbolized the waning sun, as Hekate used the torch to help guide Persephone back to Hades when the earth cooled. Then again, the torch may also represent the warming of the earth, as Hekate uses her torch to help Persephone return in the spring. Just as the sun warms the cold earth and softens before eliminating the darkness, Hekate's torches may represent renewal.

THE TORCH AS PROTECTION

The torch was also a tool of protection. It was a tool of night watchmen, who were charged with protecting a home or a city. Hekate was sometimes depicted carrying her torch with a ferocious dog at her side, both elements believed to have symbolized Hekate's role as a protector goddess.[15] If we look at Hekate's role in the Persephone and Demeter myth, Hekate may also be a protector of the lost and the bereaved. It may be that the torch is a source of power and protection.

LEADING THE WAY TO HEALING

If Persephone represents youth, innocence, and innocence lost, and Demeter represents the caring and nurturing parental archetype, Hekate may represent age and the wisdom it offers, a virtue able to transform grief and sorrow into the gold of knowledge.[16] In a purely symbolic form, the underworld may not be a physical place but rather a representation of the deeper layers of the mind, where memories and feelings are buried, perhaps those that happened to us in our youth, just as Persephone suffered trauma as a young person.

Demeter's grief may represent the sorrow or depression that we can suffer as adults if these things are not addressed. In that case, Hekate's torches serve as a guide for us to reunite with the parts of ourselves we used to be before we suffered the injury. In this role, Hekate's torches light the way toward healing.

THE MAGICK OF THE TORCH

The torch may have been a symbol of magick and may have symbolized powers to avert an evil attack.[17] In Euripides's play *Helen*, the character Menelaus invokes Hekate: "O, torch-bearing Hekate, send visions that are favorable," which may suggest that Hekate's torch may have been associated with prophecy. He later calls for Hekate's goodwill, asking that spirits from the underworld not confuse his vision or plague his existence, which may also indicate that Hekate as torchbearer is one who could be enticed to protect the petitioner from fear and hurt, but also help the person to "see" the clear nature of a situation.

Typically a symbol of the underworld, which was its own place of magick, Hekate's torches may suggest power over the dead. It's also been suggested that extinguishing a torch was believed to chase away Hekate. Although she's not specifically named, a fragment from another Euripides passage shows women attempting to expel a malevolent goddess, who was assumed to be Hekate, through a purification rite that involved extinguishing a torch.[18]

HEKATE'S USE OF THE TORCH

Hekate's torches provides light that illuminates uncertain paths, both literal and figurative, a symbol that can be thought to also bring wisdom.[19] The torch itself was a sign of revelation in the ancient world.

The *Chaldean Oracles* were referred to as "the Gnosis of the Fire," a creative fire that never consumes.[20]

In a philosophical tradition discussed in the *Chaldean Oracles*, Hekate and fire are frequently found together: Hekate receives and forms ideas via fiery lightning, nurtures them in her womb, then gives birth to them in physical form. This physical form may be expressed through the inspiration of mortals, a process sometimes called "the giver of life-bearing fire." A curse tablet referring to Hekate suggested that she originated from this great, inspirational fire.[21] (Curse tablets were frequently associated with Hermes, Persephone, and Hekate. These were essentially letters to the dead, asking for their assistance in thwarting an enemy or competition. They could be quite grisly in nature and certainly left no mercy for the intended victim of the tablet.) In this view, the torch may be a sign of passions alight, not just in desire and love, but also in rage and fury. Just as life and death have but a thin line between them, so too do love and hate, rage and elation, desire and repulsion; all are two sides of the same face. Hekate's approaching Demeter with a torch may suggest more than a simple tool of practicality; it may also symbolize the feelings of extreme desire to find Persephone.

Hekate's torch is sometimes said to "shine on two sides," which may symbolize both the mysteries of the underworld, the realm of the dead, and the miracles of the upper world, the world of the living or the world of the gods.[22] The torches may also represent life, vitality, perfection, or virtue.[23] Today, we could also embrace this symbolism with Maslow's hierarchy of needs, in which the base needs are food, shelter, and basic things that keep a body active and protected. At the top of the pyramid is self-actualization, in which a person embraces their full potential. In this lens, the torches may represent both sides of this very human scale of need and achievement.

The torches are also viewed as sparking an idea, serving as an intermediary between humanity and the divine, and potentially leading others beyond the mortal world into unknown territory.[24] In mythology, this sort of journey may represent the land of the dead, as it did for Persephone, but it may also include the unconscious and the psyche—essentially, embarking on a journey to find oneself. As Hekate is also sometimes called "the goddess of all that has been rejected," the torch may symbolize a person finding their community or embracing their identity.[25]

In many depictions, the torch highlights Hekate's role as a guide.[26] In one instance, Hekate walks in front of Persephone while looking back and down at the goddess as she holds two torches. On the right, Demeter regally awaits her daughter while Persephone looks past Hekate toward her mother. Also present is Hermes, the messenger of the gods who is also known to help characters travel back and forth from the land of the dead. Hekate does not lead Persephone all the way back from Hades, but rather takes the task from Hermes at the transition from the underworld to earth. Her backward gaze suggests she is a more than a guide; she is an attentive presence in the maiden goddess's world.[27] The torch, among many things, may represent a changing of the seasons, her role as protective guide during a frightening time, and being the lead during a transition.

THE WITCH AND THE TORCH

Hekate's torch may have been linked with Witches or other sorts of magick workers far back into antiquity. The burning torches are thought to have symbolized priests and priestesses of Hekatean mystery cults, and they were frequently used in their rites. It's possible that the use of torches might have symbolized Hekate being their patron goddess, but their use may have been simple practicality, if these rites were practiced at night. Some writings suggest that torches were a sign of an initiate being accepted into a Hekatean cult.[28] Whether these torches were a tool of the actual initiatory rite, a symbol of being initiated, or both is unknown. Another Hekatean rite included an evening race on horseback with lit torches in hand, followed by an all-night celebration. Some argue that Hekate's connection with the horse originates in this rite.[29]

In one offering made to both Hekate and Artemis at full moon festivals, small cakes were sometimes decorated with small torches, or formed crossroads offerings dedicated to Hekate.[30] Offerings to the gods in general were often burned, which may lead us to believe that goddesses associated with fire and torches, such as Hekate, were intermediaries to the gods, perhaps assisting in ferrying the sacrifices and offerings for whom they were intended.

In an image on a jug in the British Museum, Hekate (or one of her priestesses) is depicted as dancing wildly before an altar with torches in her hand, her hair flowing and her feet bare. This is a magickal rite, an ancient image of a Witch.[31]

For years, I've always felt I needed my hair and my feet bare when doing magick. On the last full moon, I went outside to collect some moon water to give to Hekate. I felt the need to use some ocean water I'd collected during an incoming tide. When I collected the water, I didn't know what I was to do with it, as is often the case with magick supplies. But as is also often the case with magick work, the purpose became clear when the time was right. I felt that Hekate wanted me to use it in a full moon rite!

Collecting moon water means taking a bowl of water and catching the reflection of the full moon in it, a feat that sounds easier than it actually is. The sky must be clear, and you must find the right angle and position to hold the bowl so that the reflection is adequately captured. It was very dark in our yard last night. I should have worn shoes. My husband had recently cut down several trees, so the ground was littered with branches and wood. Our yard is also where our puppy relieves himself, so there were quite a few droppings. But because I work my Witchcraft while barefoot, I braved splinters and poo in the dark. Fortunately, the moon was full enough to light my way—like a torch—so I did not cut my feet or step in a smelly mess. I came inside cold but wildly attuned to the night's energies. That night, I dreamed of Hekate, who suggested I bathe in the water to alleviate a particularly frustrating situation, which I did the following day. It was part of a long-term spell, so I don't yet know how it manifested. Perhaps it'll be a tale for a future book!

THE WITCH'S TORCH

Witchcraft takes us into strange situations, making us receptacles for strange tales. We are trusted with others' secrets. As a professional Witch and Tarot reader, I have had people share with me things they are deeply ashamed of, things they didn't believe they could tell another soul. I'm far from the only Witch who has experienced this. Witches help others find a way to stop fearing thoughts, feelings, or uncanny experiences. We guide people through dark times. But first, we must walk ourselves through our own dark path. Sometimes this means going at things alone. Sometimes this means seeking someone stronger than we are to walk beside us. When Persephone fulfills her bargain and agrees to stay with Hades for a portion of the year, Hekate is her guide and caretaker, perhaps her sole light in a period of darkness. When Demeter was deep in grief, it was Hekate who helped her. Hekate's comfort in the darkness helped the sad goddess be a light to others. A Witch does not have to love the darkness, but they must be at least familiar, even if not comfortable, with darkness before they too can hold a torch for another.

When I was running a coven, I often ran into "comfort culture," in which people didn't want to participate in anything in which they weren't fully comfortable. Consumer culture, which focuses on customizing everything for everyone, has led many to expect comfort in every situation. However, declaring "I'm uncomfortable" is a quick way to remove ourselves from a magickal process. What exercise strengthens our bodies if we don't experience occasional discomfort? The phrase "blood, sweat, and tears," referring to the effort put into a work project, certainly doesn't elicit the feelings of being comfortable and cozy. Likewise, most magick will have moments of modest discomfort. *An important note:* Moderate discomfort does not mean consenting or agreeing to something where you are morally or personally compromised, such as being pressured to be sexually intimate, taking substances, being forced to do things that put your physical or mental health in jeopardy, or performing a type of Magick that runs counter to your personal morals. Just as in exercise, there is a fine line between discomfort and damaging pain. Take the time to recognize the difference, to brave the former but refuse the latter.

Examples of moderate, but appropriate, discomfort might be taking part in a park cleanup when you'd rather not, singing in front of a group even if you don't like your singing voice, or leading a ritual when your preferred place is away from the spotlight. Other things that many Witches find uncomfortable include meditation, working with new forms of divination, and reading new mythologies. Witches need to routinely go to places that are uncomfortable to learn more about magick and themselves, which is its own descent into darkness. Sometimes, that uncomfortable place is literally dark.

Earlier this year, I cast a spell with two of my Witch friends, at night, on the Oregon coast. It was *very* dark, which was uncomfortable because we risked struggling to find our way home. It was also cold and wet. Yet the magick we made was powerful and effective, and I think the adverse conditions played a part in that. But sometimes the darkness we traverse is symbolic. When a friend was in a serious car accident and had a long stay in the hospital, she asked me to visit, for counsel as much as company. She was looking for how she could sustain herself emotionally during the limbo of being stuck in the hospital for so long. I didn't have the answers, but I sat with her while she figured them out on her own. It was uncomfortable, as I wished I had the answers. I wished I could fix her problem. It was uncomfortable to simply sit and listen, while also knowing that simply sitting and listening was the best I could offer. Sometimes, this is one of the most important roles of being a Witch. We shouldn't fool ourselves into thinking it's possible to have a solution for every problem. Every Witch's power has limits. Hekate didn't have the power to release Persephone, but she could stand there with a lit torch while the maiden was confined to the darkness.

WALKING WITH THE TORCHBEARER

Persephone's descent may not be into death but into embodied life—another concept that may be illustrated by Hekate's torches.[32] In many Witchcraft traditions, Witches undergo a symbolic death and rebirth. It has been my experience that entering a life of magick will invite a period of uncomfortable but ultimately productive upheaval. One of my teachers says that "the first thing magick changes is the self." When I first embraced Witchcraft as my path, my entire life course changed. I'd focused on theater arts for many years and was one semester from graduating when I realized that I wanted to be a writer instead of an actress. When I got deeper into Witchcraft and dedicated myself to a deity, a dead-end relationship evaporated overnight. Several other friendships I thought I depended on also fell apart. I thought I was heartbroken, but in truth I was liberated. Within a few months of those endings, new beginnings appeared. I met my husband and gelled with wonderful, strong friendships that I still cherish today.

Sometimes, we may find ourselves like Persephone, frightened or in a place of uncertainty. There may not be anyone around who can comfort or even be present with us. In those moments, I have called upon Hekate and her torches.

Not long ago, a hard night snuck up on me during a work trip to New York. I have a routine when I travel to the city, staying in the same hotel and eating in the same Mediterranean restaurant on my first night. The place is almost always nearly empty, a blessing in a city strangled with crowds. The staff always seats me at the same table. I bring a book instead of a screen. That night, while eating cold eggplant and grilled octopus, I read a book that detailed its author's descent into drugs and alcohol. It led me to think about an old friend whose friendship I'd set aside because of her own substance issues. I suddenly missed her terribly. There's a special sort of pain in missing a person who is so far gone that you can't touch them; when they're lost in a shell of themselves, and that shell is fractured, sharp, and hurtful.

It was a dark moon: Hekate's night. I wanted to honor Hekate, but I was also tired from my journey and suddenly emotional. I'd planned to bring my Hekate plaque with me for a makeshift altar to meditate at before bedtime, but in the chaos of last-minute packing, I'd forgotten it. I felt like a crap Witch. Yet, if there's anything I've learned from Witchcraft it is that sometimes when we're feeling our least magickal we can cast the most powerful spells.

The server asked if I wanted dessert. I didn't, but they had crème brûlée made with Turkish coffee and they would let me take it to go.

I thought of the dark moon rites of ancient Greece in which meals would be left at a three-way crossroads in honor of Hekate, in the hopes that a hungry person would come across them and be fed. I took the crème brûlée to a small park in the middle of the avenue. New York City is mostly a grid, but the streets occasionally create triangular parks, little places of respite amidst the intensity of the streets. This one was the perfect crossroads, right outside the restaurant.

I sat down on a cold bench, the early summer sky still blue as night crept in. I thought about my friend. A Witch herself, we had circled together many years before. She loved Hekate, I recalled. Maybe she still did. I began to pray.

Hekate, please watch over her. She wouldn't listen to me. Maybe she'll listen to you. Show her the way through the darkness, show her the torch where she can follow your way. Help her out of hell, or at least be by her side should she make a further descent.

I ended it with the most powerful word in magick or prayer: *Please.*

I left the dessert, wrapped and bagged neatly, on the bench so that whoever needed it would find it and eat well. I went back to my hotel room and suddenly felt compelled to call another old friend. We hadn't spoken in nearly two years, but he confessed he too had been recently thinking of our friend, although they were also no longer in touch. I cried. He listened. At the end of our conversation, I felt better.

I had asked Hekate to light the way for my ill friend. In turn, she found me someone who could light my way, too.

But Hekate wasn't done with me. It was as if she said, *You miss her, huh? Let's go see her . . .*

The following night, I ran into that old friend. We had a tearful reunion that quickly turned painful and ended with a final goodbye. I wished her well. As I walked away from her on that warm night, the glow of the subway sign a torch in the dark, the one that would take me to my hotel, I knew my friend would be all right, but that our paths had gone in different directions.

Where there had previously been darkness in the form of mystery and longing, I had been given a guide for my sorrow, and then the light into the truth of the situation. While it wasn't comfortable, it allowed me to move forward in peace, which is the greatest gift Witchcraft can offer.

WORKING WITH THE TORCHBEARER

The following spells and rituals may help you bring the power of the Torchbearer into your life. This aspect of Hekate is particularly helpful when things are uncertain. They can also be used to lend light to someone going through a tough time.

A Ritual to Invoke the Torchbearer

This rite is best done on the full moon.

Take or make an effigy of Hekate and set it on a piece of dark cloth. Circle the effigy with three candles of a color of your choosing. Consider making an offering of wine or grape juice and a pomegranate.

Say the following aloud three times, once as you light each candle:

As Demeter cried for Persephone,
As Persephone cried for Demeter,
So I cry to Hekate,
Hekate! Torchbearer! Light the way! Light the way!

When all three candles are lit, meditate on the specific areas of your life that need illumination. Then draw, journal, or envision what those areas would look like.

Place the pomegranate at a crossroads after your rite. Leave the drawing or journal entry, if you created one, in your sacred Hekate space until the next full moon.

A Prayer to Care for a Loved One while They Are Far Away

This prayer can be used at any time in the lunar cycle.

Hekate, light their way,
While they are far from my love and my care,
Hold them in your heart as I hold them in mine.
Until the darkness lifts,
Be the light in the cold dark,
Show them the way to the warmth and the light
Where my arms shall wait to receive them.
Hail, Hekate, hail the torchbearer.
May it be so.

A Spell to Guard the House and Home

Akin to the old Witch's bottles, draw or print out a picture of Hekate carrying torches. On the image, write three times:

Hekate, defend me and mine, mine and me.

Roll up the paper and insert it into a glass bottle. Consider adding personal curios such as hair or fingernail clippings, or saliva. If you can include the hair of a black dog, that's a nice touch as well. You may also consider adding shards of glass, nails, or a piece of barbed wire.

Bury the bottle beneath or near your front stoop on a dark moon. If you do not have a front stoop, consider burying it in a plant by your front door.

A Charm to Get through the Darkness

Take a stone (quartz or citrine is fine, as is a pebble found in a yard or park) and leave it in a glass of water under a waxing moon for three nights. Note: some stones, such as opal or selenite, dissolve in water. A quick internet search can tell you if your chosen stone is safe to soak in water. If your stone would be damaged by water, omit soaking it and simply leave it where the moonlight will touch it. Be sure that the water reflects the moon for at least a brief while. Carry this stone when you need clarity, direction, or light in a dark time.

CHAPTER FOUR

Ritual, Magick, and the Crossroads

Crossroads, ghosts, dogs. The underworld, liminal spaces, ethereal realms. The world soul. Magic. She is these and so much more. Yet nine years working with and for her, I'm still not sure who she is. That's the thing about Hekate. She feels like a mystery because she embodies life, death, and rebirth. She keeps me guessing and searching, making me go beyond and deeper within. Maybe someday I'll fully grasp her, maybe I won't. She stands with me when I serve as a doula as though at the gates of life and death with her torches in hand, communicating the information that I need to help bring babies into this world. Most times we embrace life. Sometimes, we journey through death. She stands with me, shedding her light as I celebrate others' victories and triumphs, and when I help them process raw emotions. She is there when I'm alone, processing rage at the things I cannot stop from happening, telling me to stay strong, to pick up the torch again, and go back to doing her work.

—TAMRHA GATTI RICHARDSON, MODERN PRIESTESS OF HEKATE

Witchcraft makes us do things that amuse, befuddle, or even frighten others who don't walk the Witch's path. Whether or not they ever involve Hekate in their craft, Witches will eventually find themselves at a personal or magickal crossroads. A helpful tool in such times is to perform a ritual with the intent to invoke illumination or direction. Such a ritual can be performed either with a group or alone. Modern Witches frequently disagree on what makes a genuine Witchcraft ritual, but Hekate's crossroads rituals are a reminder that the practice can be simple or complicated, and still greatly effective. The level of a ritual's complication depends on the nature of the magickal working as well as the Witch's abilities and resources available at the time. Hekate's crossroads also serve to remind us of the natural power contained in places other than altars or temples.

In ancient times, Hekate was believed to dwell in wild hilltops, moors, and desolate places, but also by roads, harbors, and cemeteries. In those times, a common thought was that if someone was out alone and felt suddenly afraid, it was believed their fear came from sensing Hekate's presence.[1] Other spaces sacred to Hekate included physical crossroads, especially those where three roads met. One Thessalian legend makes Hekate (as the goddess Brimo) the daughter of Pheraia, who bore her to Zeus and threw her out at the crossroads, where she was found and raised by shepherds.[2] Some say that this guise of a crossroads guardian gave Hekate her reputation as a much-feared evil spirit, one that might be encountered on the lonely road at night in a dreadful aspect, surrounded by a pack of hounds and capable of inflicting madness and nightmares.[3] Yet, as we will discover, this role at the crossroads may be more guardian than fright, more guide than devil.

Crossroads were considered liminal places, undefined and outside the rules of the world, but they also provided structure. They served a practical, worldly function as territory markers, but they also separated the worlds of the living and dead. They were frightening places, full of physical and intangible dangers. Crossroads were even considered a place where women commit murder.[4] The Greeks, Romans, and many other ancient civilizations regarded both natural and man-made liminal points (doors, gateways, rivers, and crossroads) as uncertain places that required special rituals for several different reasons. Crossroads often marked the beginning of a journey, a rite to which the Greeks and Romans assigned special significance, given that any journey outside one's home required protection. Because of their liminal reality, not being one place or another, the crossroads' identity of "sitting outside" the normal rules of the world made them feel perilous. Yet, such liminal points provided boundary and structure to the world, which prevented it from unintelligible chaos.[5]

The soil at the crossroads was considered magickal itself. Substances (plants, animals, or soils) taken from the crossroads were believed to have great power. One incantation found in Mesopotamian ruins describes an innkeeper using dust from the crossing of four roads as part of a rite to the goddess Ishtar to bring travelers and business to the door.[6] Another practice involved women in labor wearing an amulet filled with plants that grew up inside sieves thrown at crossroads to help them deliver their babies safely. People believed that burying frogs at crossroads could prevent fever.[7]

Crossroads were also where wayward spirits came together and could be summoned for protection and petition. Crossroads, perhaps as much as cemeteries, were places of great magick and, as we'll discover, were a popular place for Witches to gather to do magickal workings. This added to the general mysticism of the crossroads as well as their terror. Both aspects, as well as the crossroads themselves, were firmly in the domain of Hekate.

HEKATE AND THE CROSSROADS

Hekate was a goddess of liminality, concerned with guiding the worshipper through inherently dangerous and uncertain no-man's-land, situations that included transitions such as birth and death, as well as literal crossroads and doorways.[8] The ancient Greek playwright Aristophanes said that when a woman left her house, she made a prayer to Hekate.[9] Hekate's association with crossroads may come from her having roots foreign to the ancient Greeks. They may have seen her as a goddess who came to them from afar, and therefore associated her with spaces specifically associated with travel.

The Roman poet Ovid said, "Those who seest Hekate's faces turned in three directions that she may guard the crossroads where they branch three several ways, sometimes accompanied by ghost hounds said to serve her."[10] These three faces gave her the ability to see all that was coming simultaneously. Sometimes Hekate was depicted as three heads: one of a dog, one of a snake, one of a horse.[11]

While the torch represented a tool of protection in Hekate's hands, the crossroads represented the things she was protecting people *from*, particularly ghosts or tricky spirits, but also physical threats such as thieves or raiders. Protector images of Hekate were commonly placed at the entrance to cities, implying that she would prevent dangerous persons or elements from entering the city. Her image was also often placed before a home to guard it from evil spirits, as she had the power to both produce and control such entities. Shrines to Hekate were frequently erected at crossroads, invoking protection for travelers. These shrines may have also been potent places to seek Hekate's guidance.

Crossroads represent transitions, and Hekate was considered a patron of people experiencing different sorts of transitions. This might be simply leaving your home for work or to meet a friend, or something more serious, such as transitioning into marriage.

Hekate was an important presence in mystery cult initiations, as this event is often a sort of rebirth for the person undergoing it. Another sort of transition was that of one month to another, making the thirtieth day of each month a sacred one to Hekate.[12] Rites to Hekate may have taken place on the thirtieth of each month, and potentially at spaces where three or more roads met. Another symbolic transition under Hekate's patronage was childbirth. Hekate's triple face may have also represented a cosmological crossroads of the cosmos, earth, and the underworld, as well as the crossroads of life, death, and rebirth.[13]

For the ancient Greeks, death had its own crossroads. Passing away rarely involved a straight path. For example, without Hekate's help, an individual soul might wander between the worlds forever.[14] It was believed, however, that through purification rites and offerings at the crossroads, a positive relationship with Hekate could be formed before death, and that bond would be beneficial to the seeker at the time of their passing. A goddess connected with both the underworld and the crossroads would be perfectly suited to help souls through this transition.

CROSSROADS RITUALS

As mentioned above, the crossroads were inherently magickal and a natural space for Witches to do their work. Crossroads rituals commonly included protection, petitioning deities or spirits for assistance, devotion rites, and purification.[15] Such rituals were commonly divided into two categories: rites meant to offer protection for individuals and rites designed to release the seeker from something undesirable, such as bad luck.[16] This was a practice embraced by both individuals and communities. Corpses of those accused of particularly heinous crimes (such as murdering one's parents or other close relatives) would be thrown onto the crossroads, where citizens would hurl stones at the accused's head and/or burn the body.[17] This was likely a ritual meant to rid the city of such an act, as well as give citizens a way to release their feelings about the crime.

Perhaps in part connected to this ritual, restless ghosts were believed to haunt crossroads. It was often thought that baneful spirits were chased to and trapped at crossroads after exorcisms.[18] Suppers for Hekate or the dead were placed at crossroads on the new moon not only as a method of appeasing and averting the dead but also as a way of petitioning Hekate to keep the dead under control, particularly the souls of those who had died young.[19] These suppers were a form of purification to please the goddess as well as cleanse the soul. Crossroads were ideal spaces for magicians and Witches to work their magick, as these spirits could be used for mystical endeavors. Crossroads spirits could even be used for oracular work.[20]

THE WITCH AND THE CROSSROADS

The symbol of the crossroads and Hekate's connection to them remind Witches about the power of specific places. Naturally, working with Hekate means that physical crossroads (such as an intersection, particularly a T intersection) are particularly strong for invoking her magick. They are also good places to ask for Hekate's protection during travel or personal transitions.

Hekate's crossroads also remind us of the power of doing magick in physical locations other than our own homes. Crossroads magick gets us away from the comfort and security of our altars. My Hekate crossroads magick has prompted me to leave bulbs of garlic at the base of trees in the dark of night (with company, of course—we never want to put ourselves in danger) and walk to a three-way crossroads in the rain. Hekate has inspired me to practice magick in a state park near me that holds an unusual glacial rock formation. The walk up this hill is windy but provides a spectacular view. Best of all, it gives me the opportunity to do spellwork for blowing away negativity.

Many Witches find magick at the ocean. Others find it near rivers, on open plains, or in an urban environment. When I was living in New York City, Central Park and Inwood Hill Park were beautiful magick places, but so were the great marble lions at the New York Public Library or the enormous crossroads of Columbus Circle. The world is not short of spaces for powerful magick.

Hekate, if we let her, will help us find the right magickal places for us. Sometimes, just visiting these places, without performing any rites at all, will help us bring ourselves home to our Witchy selves, particularly in times when we have felt less magickal due to stress, trauma, or otherwise. Finding and forming a relationship with a magickal area is essential for a Witch. This is particularly important if you are unable to do magick in your own home.

THE WITCH AND THE SPIRITUAL CROSSROADS

"I'm at a crossroads in my career/relationship/life" is something I hear a lot from Tarot clients. These transitional moments often lead people to magick in the first place. Strangely enough, inviting magick into our lives will often bring us to a new place altogether, and a new perspective as we reach our next crosswords. A crossroads of my own came shortly before beginning this book, at a time when I had almost abandoned Witchcraft altogether.

While I was leading my coven and a large community attached to it, I made the mistake of believing that I could have an answer for everything. I set up expectations no person could ever fulfill, disappointing many, especially myself. It tore me down, wore me out. It had been so long since the world had felt magickal, I started to wonder if magick had ever existed at all.

Around that time, I attended a festival. It was great fun. I was happy to see so many beloved friends and share my work. But while I was surrounded by people who felt powerful things, I felt nothing. It was as though I were in a glass bubble. I could see magick happening to other people, but I couldn't connect with it myself. It made me deeply sad. On the final night of the festival, everyone gathered for the main ritual. People seemed excited, but I wasn't. I slipped away from the ritual and into the night, just as a heavy rain broke the long summer drought. I sat on the hard, wet ground and cried.

It was a dark night, a new moon. And a bit of magick returned.

Hekate was beside me. I couldn't see or hear her, but I knew she was there. I then understood that I was at a crossroads, and could see each path. I could continue down the path I was on, the one in which I was the sole source of magick for everyone else but me, but I would lose all magick, forever. Witchcraft would be a memory and I would lose a very valuable part of myself. Or, I could take a different path, one in which I placed my own magickal life before helping others (like the safety instructions on an airplane to put on your own oxygen mask before assisting others) and eventually regain the magick that I lost and missed. I chose the latter.

We are not limitless wells, but ones that must be replenished, and we must treat ourselves as our most valuable resources. That was the greatest lesson I learned from Hekate.

CROSSROADS RITES

The philosopher Apollonius (15–100 CE) said that the ancients made certain sacrifices to Hekate with ceremonies and formal tributes so special that they were dedicated to her alone. He described one such ceremony:

Pay close attention: when humid night has reached the middle of its course, seek out the waters of the river. There, after being washed in arms and hands and dressed in the deep blue garment, be mindful to dig a pit. Then at once let the lamb, a female, be slaughtered and over the pit let it be burned on the pyre. Call on Hekate, the daughter of Perses, and by honey, the sweet gift of the bees, you will please her. When these rites are completed, I warn you to depart from the pyre. Let nothing turn you back, not the trampling of feet nor the barking of dogs. For all the effort of the sacred act would be void.[21]

This gives us some insight into the rites of Hekate. It is suggested that the petitioner ritually cleanse themselves first, and dress in a dark garment. It suggests making a sacrificial offering, which in this case is a lamb, followed by an offering of honey. Lastly, the working requires turning away and not looking back, which is a commonality to Hekate work but may also be indicative of working with chthonic deities. We see something similar in the next passage, in which Medea assists her husband Jason by casting a sinister spell. Medea is known in Greek literature as a Witch and a priestess of Hekate, and in some cases a goddess in her own right:

Waiting for the mid-moment of the night's dividing, having washed thyself in the flood of the unwearied river, alone and apart and clad in somber hue, dig thee a pit well-rounded. And within it slay a she-lamb, and lay it raw and whole on a pile which thou has heaped together in the pit. Then pray to Hekate the sisterless, . . . pouring from a cup the honey of the hive-bee. When thou hast thus mindfully propitiated the goddess, get thee away back from the pyre; and let neither thud of feet nor howl of dogs tempt thee to look back, lest thou bring all to naught and thyself return not to thy comrade in any seemly wise.[22]

The author may have been inspired by other Hekate rites of the age, as Medea's working parallels the description offered by Apollonius. We also get a sense of the timing, given that the rite begins at "the mid-moment of the night's dividing," which likely means midnight. "An unwearied river" may indicate a particularly unused place of water, a place where people do not go to wash themselves, or where the water is still. "Alone and apart and in somber hue": she is by herself, likely dressed in dark clothing (perhaps blue, as suggested above), either so that she is not easily seen or because she is trying to connect with chthonic spirits, which the ancient Greeks identified with dark colors.

She digs a hole and sacrifices a female lamb, presumably for Hekate. It may be that a fire was built in this pit and the lamb offering was burnt. Burned offerings were also common in crossroads rituals. She then prays to Hekate, acknowledging that in her tradition of honoring Hekate she is invoking every solitary deity, and offering a cup of honey as well. It is in this offering that Medea petitions Hekate for assistance with her working. While it's not clear that what she is doing is at the crossroads, she does do the traditional Hekate work of turning as soon as the rite is over and walking away, being careful not to look back.

Later in the chapter, we will look at how the practices of the ancient Witches can help us shape our own magick.

CROSSROADS OFFERINGS

In addition to the typical suppers, three categories of offerings were probably left at crossroads for Hekate: katharmata, katharsia, and oxuthumia.[23] Katharmata included portions of sacrifices made at temples, which were not used in ceremony, something that included waste blood and water. Katharsia included the actual remains of sacrifices made in temples or other ritual spaces. Oxuthumia was a baked clay censor used to fumigate the house for protection, and then taken and left at the crossroads. (It's not clear whether the censor itself was left at the crossroads or if the household sweepings were taken and burned on the censor at the crossroads.)[24]

Note: Some of the sacrifices to Hekate in the ancient world are quite grisly, and I know of no modern Hekate devotees who would ever emulate them, for both legal and ethical reasons. I've included them here for informational purposes only—and as a serious dog lover, I hope no one would ever consider replicating them.

In many accounts, it is said that black puppies or other black animals were sacrificed to Hekate because the color was associated with the underworld and darkness. White animals, on the other hand, were often sacrificed to Olympian gods, perhaps assuming they were closer to the light of the sun and stars.[25] Sacrifices to Olympians happened during the day, while sacrifices to chthonian spirits happened at night.[26] These day and night associations may have fed the later assertion that things of black magick were baneful and things of white magick were good, given that many curse tablets were associated with chthonic deities. I would advise avoiding the terms black magick and white magick, because in magick work the colors black and white don't actually associate with bad or good. Also, they have overt racist connotations that are best left in the past.

Offerings were typically made in front of a god's statue. In some cases, statues in ancient Greece were washed, dressed, and ornamented with jewelry, even sometimes taken out into the wilderness and let to go on retreat.[27] Chthonian deities, such as Hekate, typically received their offerings in a cave or an adyton, which was part of a sanctuary reserved for oracles, priests, or priestesses but not available to the general public.[28] This space may have represented a tomb. Such spaces represented the worlds of the living and the dead, a crossroads itself. If you are lucky enough to live near a cave, consider leaving an offering there (so long as it is biodegradable and won't affect the ecosystem). To be on the safe side, consider leaving it at the mouth of the cave. Alternatively, leave an offering at a riverside, again keeping in mind ecological considerations. Just as the River Styx was a place of crossing from the world of the living to the dead, the river might also be considered its own kind of crossroads.

MAKING MAGICK THROUGH RITES

Many Witches recite the phrases, "It's all about your intention; if you put the intention out there, the magick will happen." This is true, to a point. If I got into my car or started walking without an intended destination, I'd drive or walk in circles. This is not to say that a periodic aimless drive or walk isn't good for one's well-being—but to get where we need to go, we need to set an intention. Likewise, I might have every intention of going to the bookstore, but if I don't get up and take the proper actions to go (dress, put on shoes, take my wallet), I will never get there. Likewise, when making magick, intention must be coupled with action. In reviewing the things Hekate's ancient Witches did to summon her work, whether at the crossroads or at other magickal spaces, we can learn a few things about making the most effective magick.

Timing

The Witches of ancient Greece focused heavily on the right time to do their Hekate magick, which was most often at midnight. Today, midnight isn't much of a silent hour, given the prevalence of electricity and variety of work schedules; but in the age of the ancient

Greeks, where people followed the cycles of the sun, midnight would have been a very quiet time indeed. Most magick requires a certain level of privacy. In this world, however, it also requires a degree of practicality. Midnight may not be practical for you, personally. While most Witches I know prefer the night to the early morning, I have found that predawn hours contain extremely potent magick.

Safety is also a serious consideration, particularly if you are doing your rites at an outdoor sacred space. When I was living in New York, I did lots of magick work in the parks, but I deliberately went there during busy times for the sake of safety, and took a friend along if I wanted to work in a more secluded area. I was careful to be nonchalant about doing my work, and generally few people noticed.

Many Witches enjoy incorporating astrological hours or tide tables into their magick. Instructions on using these are outside the scope of this book but may be worth considering when choosing a time to cast your spells.[29]

If your rites are specifically for Hekate, consider doing the work at some of these times:

- On the final day of the month.

- On a new moon.

- On a full moon. (Although the new moon may be more traditional, Hekate is connected to all lunar elements—and full moons are considered a sacred time for Witches.)

Cleansing

Hekate spells place a great emphasis on cleansing oneself before doing the work. While we may not have the full cultural context to explain why this was important in ancient Greece, we can say that in doing the magick, a cleansing routine is helpful in releasing distracting energies or otherwise before doing the work.

Several years ago, I worked at a particularly stressful job and felt anxious nearly every day. After coming home from a particularly difficult day, I threw my clothes on the floor. I slept in late the next day and enjoyed a relaxing morning with my husband, and felt very calm. Perhaps out of laziness, I put on the clothes I'd left on the floor the day before, not thinking about how they were connected to the energy of the job. Almost immediately, the anxiety returned. Because I was supposed to do magick with my coven that afternoon, I changed into clean clothes immediately, as I did not want to bring the anxious energy of the previous day into the magick we were trying to do together.

A personal energetic cleansing prior to doing magick is very helpful not just for yourself, but also for the effectiveness of your magick. It can attune your mind to the work that you want to do and release any negative energy that you don't want to bring into the magick.

Using a river for cleansing, as the spells above suggest, is impractical for many. But a cleanse with a bowl of water or a sacred bath are perfectly acceptable. Smoke can be just as cleansing as water and may be an easier option in some cases. I have included a couple of easy smoke and water cleansings at the end of the chapter. For further resources, see *Deliverance!* by Khi Armand or *Sacred Smoke* by Amy Blackthorn.

Keep in mind that the crossroads themselves may be excellent places to do personal energetic cleansing work.

Offering

While most things in magick can be left up to interpretation, making an offering is one step that shouldn't be skipped. When you make an offering to gods or spirits, you are forming a relationship with them. If you've taken the time to light candles, burn incense, or sing a song for them, that god is more likely to come to your aid.

Such crossroads offerings need not be physical. In ancient Greece, reciting poetry or singing a song in praise of the goddess being petitioned was perfectly acceptable. Theocritus presents Simoetha, who does her enchanting this way: "May you shine brightly, O Moon. To you, O Goddess, I shall pleasingly direct my songs, and to Hekate of the underworld, whom even the hounds fear."[30]

Hekate's traditional offerings included eels, mullet, bread, and honey cakes.[31] The exact composition of the honey cake is unknown, but here's a basic a recipe in case you want to make this offering to Hekate:

You will need:

- 2 cups flour

- 1 cup sugar

- ½ cup butter (one stick)

- honey

Mash all of the ingredients together and form into a round cake.

Bake at 350 degrees until golden. Remove from oven and allow to cool completely. Carefully transfer to a plate.

Cover the cake with honey and leave it as an offering at the crossroads, or along with any other offerings you'd like to give.

Consider using ingredients that you yourself like and eat. It's easy to gift items that you would not eat yourself. But it's a greater gift to give when it's hard. I have celiac and can't eat gluten. It's nothing for me to make a cake with regular flour to give to the gods. I can't consume it, anyway! But when I make something with my pricier gluten-free flour, consume nothing for myself, and leave it all for them, I am making a special sacrifice. However, if money was tight or I didn't have time to buy gluten-free ingredients but had regular flour in the house, I'd make do with what I had.

In both spells above, the writers talk about sacrificial lambs, which was a common practice in this era. There is no need to recreate this practice or any similar practice. If you'd like to offer meat as an offering to Hekate, you can purchase the meat from the grocery store, cook it, and eat it as a sacred meal in her honor, or prepare a meal to give to someone in need. Meat offerings are also not absolutely necessary; vegetarian or vegan food items are perfectly acceptable.

If you are interested in forming a relationship with Hekate, consider making routine offerings on certain days, such as the thirtieth or thirty-first day of the month, even if you are not casting a spell or asking Hekate for anything. If you are leaving your offerings at the crossroads, consider burying or burning the offering, being mindful of the environment, as this invokes the typical way that Hekate was honored and given offerings in the past.

DRESSING FOR RITUAL

Many Witches love dressing in black, but plenty of traditions use white or bright colors when working with spirits. The color you choose for your Hekate rites is less important than the significance behind why you chose the color for you, your tradition, and your ancestry. While it's not breaking any Witchcraft laws to do your magickal workings in the T-shirt and jeans you had on earlier in the day (I do it all the time), assigning a specific garment for your magickal work enhances the experience. If alternative clothes are not possible or if you don't have time to change, even draping a piece of cloth (perhaps a scarf) around your neck or head before doing the work is helpful. The point is to remove yourself from your normal routine, telling your mind and body, and the spirits around you, that you're preparing to make magick. This will open you up to better sensing the spirits around you and, whether psychologically or energetically, removing the day's distractions.

WORKING AT THE CROSSROADS OR ANY SACRED SPACE

When you do your work, remember to begin by honoring the spirits of place. If you live on land that is colonized, it's respectful to give an offering to the spirits of the original inhabitants of the land. Depending on who these people were, the proper offering may vary. If you're unsure, offering clean water to the land is always acceptable and in many cases preferable to leaving food that might sicken animals or pollute the environment.

While being mindful of your personal safety, get uncomfortable. Remember, Witchcraft is not always convenient or easy. This doesn't mean you need to go miles out of your way or into an unsafe environment, but the moments of discomfort (getting a little cold, wet, or dirty) are the ones that fully connect us with the power of magick.

DON'T LOOK BACK

It is said that one must not look back after performing crossroads work with Hekate. The earlier practitioners may have thought this was bad luck, and it may be. But the greater work is that it's part of the magickal process. After letting your magick go into the world, continuing to look at it is akin to peeking in the oven to see if the cake is rising. Hint, hint: It won't! This also includes over-consulting divination, such as through Tarot or pendulums, to see how things are going.

RELEASE THE NEED FOR PERFECTION

It won't be perfect. There will always be exceptions. Sometimes you just have to run with it.

Ordinarily, I would dress properly for where I was going, and put on shoes before leaving the house. But if the house were on fire, I would run outside in whatever I had on. And if I got a call from my boss wanting to see me immediately and I suspected it was for an uh-oh type of reason, I wouldn't have time to prepare and give a full offering at the crossroads. In these cases, consider saying a prayer to invoke Hekate's help, and perhaps gift her with something later.

If money is tight, don't skip meals or walk to work to buy a gift for the gods. Pagan gods don't require us to martyr ourselves. Never underestimate the value of singing, reciting a poem, or collecting trash at a natural space.

EMBRACING HEKATE AT THE CROSSROADS

Symbolic crossroads can be terrible things, often leaving us wondering if we should have gone one way instead of another. It's easy to fear the crossroads, and the choice we'll have to make, long before we find ourselves there. When we do reach these junctures, there's almost always a clear path forward. But there is less of a danger in making a wrong choice than in staying at the crossroads too long. The ancient Greeks may have thought that spirits would attack if you lingered too long—and maybe they would. Likewise, if we agonize over a decision for too long, our choices may start to fade away.

What is it about the place where roads meet that invites such fear and imagination? Is it because it's a point where we could easily get lost by taking the wrong road? Is it because there's an inherent sense of danger, perhaps at one time when bandits might have lurked at these crossroads, or because they were liminal spaces considered the domain of spirits? No matter the case, they represent change, and change can be scary. They represent the unknown and the mysterious. In that, they are the perfect symbol of Witchcraft, and they are a comfortable lair of Hekate.

Early into writing this book, I felt disconnected from Hekate. This was likely due to the common writer's experience of self-doubt that accompanies most writing endeavors. The warm excitement I felt when I'd first begun had quickly diminished. I made an altar for her, decorated it, and tended it faithfully. It was a pleasant experience, but I still didn't *feel* her. I took it as a sign to get up and away from the altar, and to look for her elsewhere.

Three nights in a row, the night before the new moon, the night of the new moon, and the night after, I visited a small grove of trees near a T intersection: a bona fide crossroads. On the first night, I sliced an apple into nine pieces and left them in a circle at the base of an oak tree. On the second night, I broke three bulbs of garlic into pieces and left them as an offering, too. On the third night, I left clean water. Nothing specific happened, but that space became magickal. When I passed those trees while doing errands, I felt that Hekate was nearby. Shortly thereafter, I learned that oak, in some traditions, is sacred to Hekate. The connection had been made, I realized. It just felt gentler than I had expected.

Doing magick work at the crossroads is like having coffee with Hekate. If you have specific magick in mind, doing that magick at the crossroads is good no matter what you do. If you're not sure what magick you want to do, visiting a crossroads may help clarify it. But even more so, Hekate's crossroads reminds us of one of the greatest roles of Witches. Just as Brimo was left at the crossroads, and those accused of murder were also cast to the crossroads, the world of Witchcraft embraces those who have been cast aside by mainstream society.

A Protection Spell

Draw the outline of a dog. Inside the dog's body, write down the things you feel need protection, such as your position at work, your children, your pets, your partner (or partners), an elderly family member, etc. You can even write your own name down if you need protection.

Once you've listed the things you want protected, take a black crayon and fill the entire image, covering the names and words you've written.

Fold the paper inward three times. Bury it beneath a rock at a crossroads, preferably at night. Always remember that safety is paramount. Take someone with you if need be, or know it's also fine to do this work during the day.

A Ritual to Release Negativity from House or Home

This is inspired in part by the ancient Greeks' tradition of purifying the house just before or after childbirth, or to purify the house of ghosts, combined with elements of American Hoodoo.

Starting at the back of your home, sweep all the dirt to the front and collect it. Remove any plastic bits or other pieces that will not biodegrade. Take the sweepings to the crossroads, and while your back is turned to the intersection throw them over your shoulder. Walk home and do not turn around or look behind you until you return home.

In the following days, return to the crossroads to leave Hekate an offering of thanks, such as apples or a bulb of garlic.

A Prayer to Help You Navigate a Crossroads

When you are at your own crossroads and don't know which choice to make, offer this prayer first thing in the morning and just before bedtime:

> Gracious lady of the crossroads,
> Torchbearer, key keeper,
> Guide me as I walk this path.
> Light my way, guard my walk,
> Unlock the gate to my best destiny.

Consider carrying a pinch of soil collected from a nearby crossroads while you are deliberating your decision. When you have made a choice, return the soil to the crossroads along with a biodegradable offering to Hekate.

CHAPTER FIVE

Goddess of Ghosts

Its blackish sap, like the ooze from a mountain oak,
she'd gathered, to make her drug with, in a Kaspian seashell,
after bathing first in seven perennial freshets,
and seven times calling on Brimo—roarer and rearer,
Brimo, night-wanderer, chthonian sovereign over
the dead—on a moonless night, wrapped in a black mantle.
—APOLLONIOS RHODIOS, *THE ARGONAUTIKA*[1]

Ancient Athenian funeral rites were grim affairs. The ancient Greeks believed there was little hope for joy in an afterlife. Death was not complete oblivion for the individual, but the conventional notions of afterlife offered minimal comfort for the dying or bereaved. While the greatest heroes and souls were believed to experience an exception, the majority of souls were taken by the god Hermes to the underworld for an eternity in a shadowy and unpleasant existence ruled by the cold gods Hades and Persephone. One of Hekate's symbols, the whip, was a symbol of power in the underworld, and potentially one used to control or even punish the souls of the deceased.[2] Because of this, the living had no concern about being rewarded or punished in the afterlife for actions done while alive. One could be pious and kind or craven and cruel, but all were still likely to end up in the dreary realm of Hades.

Perhaps because of this belief in a morbid afterlife, rites of grief were demonstrated at annual visits to gravesites. These visits included sacrifices appropriate to the underworld, which often included food, as there seemed to be concern about the dead going hungry.[3] Hungry, bored, or disrespected ghosts were believed to haunt the living, so proper appeasement was essential.

The ancient Greeks not only believed that ghosts existed, but they considered them a constant threat. Even the spirit of a beloved family member could potentially bring illness, misfortune, or even death to living relatives. Intricate rites designed to appease the dead or prevent them from returning were a routine part of life. Described as a goddess from whom even the most ferocious dogs cowered as she walked among the graves, Hekate could protect the living from potentially harmful, restless spirits or encourage such spirits to cause problems for the living.[4] A healthy relationship with Hekate was vital in keeping the dead at a safe distance.

At the same time, the dead could be helpful. The dangerous dead could be employed by Witches to aid in spellcasting. Cemeteries, like crossroads, were powerful spaces to perform Witchcraft. The ancient Greeks believed both that the dead lingered near the grave *and* that the soul escaped the earthly realm, residing both in the tomb and in Hades, much as many modern Christians believe the soul can rest both in a tomb and in heaven. Descriptions of some ancient Greek funeral rites suggest that the newly dead could hear the living and receive offerings, potentially to do the bidding of the living.[5] To solicit the services of these dead, ghosts would need to be nourished before they could interact with the living.[6] Hekate's suppers at the crossroads not only helped keep the dead from disaffecting the living but also potentially appeased and attracted them to a cause. It was likely believed that Hekate could be persuaded to keep the dead locked in the underworld so that they wouldn't be a bother to anyone, or release them so that they could help a Witch with a spell.

Cemeteries were a fertile place for all sorts of magick, but particularly more baneful, or harmful, magick. This magick, along with the basic, natural terror of cemeteries, may have helped shaped the more sinister aspects of Hekate's reputation.

HEKATE AND THE DEAD

As a periodic intermediary between the world of gods and that of men, Hekate served as a messenger spirit between the living and the dead. But this role was considered as fearsome as it was helpful. Hekate was often shown haunting the underworld as a monstrous female figure accompanied by dogs. Her association with the dark moon either represented or further solidified her relationship with the underworld, particularly ghosts and demons, given that the dark moon had chthonic connections.[7] In one translation of her name as "a hundred," she was believed to possess the power of compelling the ghosts of the unburied dead, who would otherwise wander for one hundred years.[8] Hekate was also said to send forth demons and spirits by night from the underworld, to dwell in tombs or near the blood of murdered persons, and to teach sorcery and Witchcraft at the crossroads to those brave enough to seek her.[9] Even in Shakespeare's *Macbeth*, the Witches, who worshipped and worked for Hekate, summoned a variety of dead to parade before Macbeth, both comforting and alarming him. It was believed if someone suffered from nightmares, they had been attacked by Hekate or an agent of hers.[10] It was said that on moonless nights, Hekate circled graves while carried on the backs of her dogs, attended by those who had died young.[11] It was thought that if someone were possessed by spirits or terrors that struck at night, particularly with ailments that drove them out of bed, Hekate was responsible, having invaded the body of the afflicted.[12]

Hekate was believed to control the actions of the dead. Certain dead were a particular threat, such as the unburied or those who had died young, who could grow angry and might seek to harm the living—two classes of deceased over whom Hekate had special patronage.[13] Honoring Hekate might have been instrumental in the ability of the living to appease and protect themselves from vengeful dead. It was common to place an image of Hekate at the threshold of a home to prevent ghosts from entering.[14]

Some argue that Hekate has always had connections to the dead, and that it was her connection with Witchcraft, rather than death, that gave her a sinister reputation, as Witches have been infamous for centuries.[15] Nevertheless, Hekate's relationship with the dead was not one of eternal peace, but one associated with humanity's greatest fears around death. While Hekate had control over all the dead, she was especially connected with the recently deceased, along with souls who died untimely, violent, or unnatural deaths, or those who were denied proper burial rites. These spirits included murderers, whose bodies were often left at crossroads. Her alternative name of Brimo suggests a furious, disorderly goddess from the depths of the earth, a "sovereign over the dead," one traditionally known for roaming graveyards with her band of restless ghosts and demons.[16]

But Hekate was not always known as a goddess of ghosts. Prior to the fifth century, Hekate was described as a benevolent goddess. Toward the end of the fifth century, writers began categorizing Hekate as a malevolent goddess of ghosts, Witchcraft, and sorcery who could, and would, occasionally harm people—particularly women in childbirth or newborns. The reason for the switch is unclear. It's possible that world events (famine, war, or natural disasters) shaped

Hekate's reputation from benevolent to sinister, or invoked a greater belief in and fear of ghosts. After the Civil War in the United States, beliefs in ghosts and hauntings skyrocketed, possibly in reaction to massive numbers of anonymous dead buried without socially acceptable funeral rites, a situation that would have unnerved the living.[17] Likewise, situations in which the dead received less than ideal care may have spurred belief and fear in ghosts for the Greeks and their contemporaries. It may also be that the Greeks absorbed beliefs of other cultures who had a stronger fear of ghosts and chthonic deities like Hekate. Then again, it's possible that the writings depicting Hekate as a beautiful and generous goddess reflected certain authors' personal interpretations and did not accurately reflect their contemporaries' opinions of Hekate.[18]

Today, death goddesses such as Hekate are enjoying a resurgence in popularity. This may reflect modern feelings about death. Due to medical advances and a more abundant food supply, people are living longer. Death is often, and perhaps reasonably, assumed to be something that will happen "someday," and not a consistent, lurking threat in the way it was to older civilizations. Today, the dead and dying are often hidden from view, making death more mysterious. Alternatively, with the instability of so many other parts of modern life, such as climate change and a global rise in fascism, death may be experiencing some fetishizing.

No matter the relationship of either ancient or modern Witches to ghosts, Hekate's relationship with the dead highlights the fears of and relationships to the greatest mystery in life: what happens when we die. Modern Witches honoring Hekate may experience further layers. By inviting Hekate into our lives, will we be confronted with difficult memories? Will we need to look at parts of ourselves that horrify us? Inviting any deity into our lives, particularly one such as Hekate, will always provide such an opportunity for uncomfortable introspection. But such goddesses also offer helpful magickal tools. To identify them, it's first helpful to look at what the underworld, and the ghosts that inhabit it, could offer to ancient Witches.

HEKATE RITES OF THE DEAD

Hekate was an important part of ancient Greek rites honoring the dead. The meals (or "suppers") of cakes, garlic, mullet, eggs, cheese, and sprats that were commonly left at crossroads as offerings to Hekate invited her protection against the restless ghosts believed to frequent crossroads. It was considered dangerous to come across these meals, and even more dangerous to consume them, the thought being that the dead would curse someone who encountered their meals. Should someone come across a person feasting on such food at crossroads, they would leave the area quickly, pour water over their head, and summon a priestess to carry a quill or puppy round them for purification, which would banish any polluting powers.[19] It may also have been believed that the person eating the food might be possessed by the dead, or even be a ghost themselves—even further reason to avoid such sights.

Both Hekate and the dead were consulted for purification and protection. Her connection with the dog was emblematic of her role in death and the underworld. In some magickal papyri, Hekate, known as a dog-lover and leader of dog packs, and invoked while dogs howl, howls like a dog herself.[20] She was also sometimes called "the bitch" or "she-wolf."[21]

Dogs themselves were considered agents of the dead. In addition to being killers in certain conditions, they were scavengers, literal eaters of the dead, who howled in the night, the time when people were most likely to either pass away or see their illnesses worsen. But dogs were also revered as natural protectors, particularly of the home. One statue of Hekate at Byzantium (what is now Istanbul, Turkey) commemorated the good service of the dogs who aroused the citizens of the colony when they were attacked by night.[22] Because of their scavenger nature, dogs may have gained their association with both purification and with the dead by consuming offerings left in rites meant to honor or abate the dead, essentially cleansing the space. They were also able to consume foul energy from humans.[23] For this reason, it was considered good to invoke Hekate and her hounds in haunted places and crossroads for her protection against baneful or restless spirits.

It can be safely assumed that Hekatean rites of the dead were quite prevalent in ancient Greece. One way to tell how powerful a belief or practice might have been is to look for the voices who spoke out against it. In the final book of the New Testament, the early Christian church seems to note the powerful presence of both Hekate and the associated rites of the dead through their admonishment against them:

> Blessed are those who wash their robes, so that they may have the right to the tree of life and may enter the city by its gates.

> But outside are the dogs, the sorcerers, the sexually immoral, the murderers, the idolaters, and everyone who loves and practices falsehood. (Revelation 22:14–15)

These verses highlight a common funeral practice of the time, which was to strip the clothes from the corpse, wash them, and dress the corpse in clean white robes as a prelude to being carried out. The mourners in some regions also wore white robes. These verses may be a warning against the cult of Hekate and her dogs, a cult concerned with spirits of the dead, particularly when looking at the connection to dogs and murderers (who were buried at Hekate's sacred place of the crossroads).[24] The very fact that these practices were highlighted and warned against by the verse's author likely underscores their prevalence.

WITCHCRAFT WITH THE DEAD

Given that crossroads were places where the dead gathered as well as where household garbage was often taken, it's possible that the dead were believed to play a part in purification rites at crossroads. Cemeteries were also active places for Witchcraft. One such act involved the use of the curse tablet.

It's possible that a lack of belief in a pleasant afterlife accounted for the use of lead curse tablets.[25] The ancient Greeks may have believed that their dead were bored and therefore willing to help a living person with a magickal endeavor. A spirit with a reason for being restless might be preferable to employ for a spell so they would not be inclined to haunt. Witches looking for help from the dead particularly preferred the restless souls of young or untimely dead.[26] Hekate, in her role as a guardian and guide of such ghosts, was frequently invoked before casting, as she could deliver these souls to the conjurer.

Curse tablets were placed in underground sanctuaries and/or sources of water, graves, or any other location that offered contact with the dead, particularly the recent or untimely dead. Such unsettled souls might more readily carry the message down to the underworld, where the result would be wrought.[27] The spell's victim would be bound and restricted in their endeavors by the souls invoked by the Witch's workings.[28]

The curse tablets covered a wide range of issues: legal and political disputes, commercial rivalry, and sexual matters, such as attracting a lover or cursing a rival. It's sometimes thought that the dead were consulted for matters in which two people were competing and only one could win, such as a chariot race, a court case, or a love affair.[29] One such curse reads:

> Let Pherenicus be bound before Hermes Chthonios and Hekate Chthonia . . . I bind before them Galene [the name of a prostitute], who is associated with Pherenicus. And just as the lead is held in no esteem and is cold, so may Pherenicus and his things be held in no esteem and be cold, and so for the things which Pherenicus' collaborators say and plot concerning me.

> Let Thersilochus, Oenophilos, Philotios and any other legal advocate of Pherenicus be bound before Hermes Chthonios and Hekate Chthonia. And I bind the soul and mind and tongue and plans of Pherenicus, whatever he does and plots concerning me, let all things be contrary for him and for those who plot and act with him.[30]

We can gather that the author was threatened, or at least bothered, by Pherenicus, enough to wish ill on not only Pherenicus but everyone associated with him. It's possible Pherenicus was a brothel owner, and the spellcaster might have been his competition, possibly another sex worker or brothel owner. The creation of this spell tablet was likely expensive, and to maximize its effects the spellcaster made sure to mention everyone who might be a threat either at the time or in the future.

A collection of curse tablets found in 2003 involves Hekate, Artemis, and Hermes and targets a couple who ran a tavern, with commercial rivalry as the most likely motive for casting the spell.[31] Some of the tablets describe ritual actions employed during the cursing process: chanting, wax figures, yarn, and bits of hair and clothing (possibly those of the person being cursed). These rituals were likely dynamic and personal and not bound to any sort of orthodoxy.[32] One spell from the collection is written as follows:

> Hekate Chthonia, Artemis Chthonia, Hermes Chthonios,
> cast your hate upon [name]
> and their endeavor, power, possessions.
> I will bind my enemy [name], in blood and ashes
> with all the dead. Nor will the next four-year cycle release you.
> I will bind you in such a bind as strong as is possible.
> And I will smite down on your tongue.[33]

Curse tablets left no room for error. The above tablet refers to a four-year cycle in which the curse cannot be lifted, later listing an array of other underworld deities who were not allowed to loosen the curse under even the most tempting of circumstances.[34] These curse tablets were used not only as a means of righting wrongs but also as a way to subdue competition. Such curse tablets could be found among educated and wealthy members of society, suggesting that this practice was more than fringe superstition; it was a well-recognized rite within the faith and culture, crossing economic and other demographic backgrounds.[35]

Some of these spells may make some modern Witches uncomfortable, as many do not believe cursing or using magick to manipulate a situation is ethical. However, we must consider the context. Religious and spiritual practices tend to become extreme when the practitioners experience an extreme environment. The above curse tablets were created and used during a period historically dominated by war and shifting political alliances.[36] It's likely that baneful curses came out of desperation, not maliciousness.

THE WITCHES DOING THE WORK

Graveside spellcastings were common, and curse tablets were often deposited by mourners during mortuary rituals either at or immediately after the burial, usually by a family member or other close relation.[37] It may have been believed that the newly dead could better hear the requests of the living than those who had passed on long before. Maybe the newly dead would bring the petitions as they descended to the underworld, where the intention could more quickly manifest. Or the goal may be to give the recently deceased something to do in their afterlife so that the spirit would not become restless and potentially haunt the living.

Women maintained tombs and performed graveside rites for dead relations. Because women frequently accessed the grave, they were likely the ones to leave the curse tablets. In matters dealing with fiscal success, husbands, wives, and potentially dependents (slaves and children) worked together in supernatural undertakings. Curses that targeted couples or businesses could be considered a household or workplace affair, potentially requiring several members of the household or workplace to take part in the deposit.[38]

A key rule of magick is that it must be carried out in secret, lest it be interrupted by others with conflicting agendas. A woman could secretly carry out the plot, making it look as though she were tending a grave when she was actually depositing a tablet that cursed a rival. It's likely that these acts were carried out at night, possibly on new moons, when less light would be conducive to secrecy. Given that the new moon, the dead, and the cemetery were all domains of Hekate, she was surely important to the process.

Nighttime was when phantoms roamed the earth, and Hekate, as goddess of the restless spirits, roamed with her hellhounds. Witches would have performed their most dangerous magick at this time, out of sight and with the help of Hekate and her servant spirits.

As Shakespeare's Macbeth considers the particulars of the murder he will commit, he notes that the night is dark and made for Witches' prophecies, as well as Hekate:

... Now o'er the one half world
Nature seems dead, and wicked dreams abuse
The curtain'd sleep; witchcraft celebrates
Pale Hecate's offerings, and wither'd Murder,
Alarum'd by his sentinel, the wolf,
Whose howl's his watch . . .[39]

Dark, night, secrecy, the grave. These are the domains of Hekate. They are frightening, but they have an important place in living. For Witches, we must become familiar with these things, even if we never love them.

LIVING GHOSTS: LESSONS IN THE DARK

While I was working on the first draft of this chapter, my dog woke me up long before dawn. I didn't know the time, as we were having a blackout, and I could not see the numbers on my alarm. I may be a Witch, but that doesn't mean I'm not afraid of the thin, pitch-black hours of the morning. But the puppy needed to go out, and I didn't want to clean up an accident. I prayed to Hekate to keep any ghosts at bay and focused on what was immediately ahead of me—finding my way to the back door.

The dark offered a gift: pure quiet. Because of the blackout, not a single appliance had power. Without the hum of the fridge or the heater, I could appreciate the peace of predawn, a kind of quiet so deep I could lie in it for a month. I also found that once my eyes adjusted, I could see better without a flashlight. The bright beam made things even scarier, casting greater shadows than if I simply let the dark be as it was. I learned a few things from that night: Not all darkness needs light; sometimes it's best to let it alone. Also, when we're most afraid, focusing on the task at hand rather than our fears helps us traverse them with ease. Hekate's answer to my prayer that night came with the reminder of the gift in the darkness. It's not always a problem to solve. Periods of dark can, if we let them, allow us to see things differently and perhaps identify our most pure intention.

There is another kind of darkness that Hekate can take us into: the darkness in ourselves. Sometimes we need to revisit our own ghosts—exorcising some, using others. I myself experienced this a few years ago, when I was not a new Witch but I was still a new priest-ess. This was when I still lived in New York. I'd recently reconnected with an old boyfriend who lived in a different state. Many years prior, we'd dated several times. It always ended for different reasons, most of which were rooted in us being young and unsure of what we wanted from each other, but they usually involved me accusing him of not taking me, or my passions, seriously enough. But we'd matured, we thought. We should give it one more try. He came to visit just before Halloween. I dragged him through underground clubs, burlesque performances, a famous haunted house, and a photo shoot. We even prepared for my coven's Halloween ritual together. I told him, and myself, that I was giving him an unforgettable New York experience. In retrospect, I was testing him. Could he handle me and all I had become? Would he finally respect my passions?

Through it all, he smiled and took it in, patiently and quietly. He didn't seem to judge. He just seemed to be enjoying his own experience.

Halloween rituals, which were designed for participants to honor their dead, were intense, cathartic experiences for my coven. Many believed they were sharing the space not only with their beloved dead but also with Hekate herself, as we would ritually trance her into someone who could speak on behalf of the goddess.[40] No matter how a Witch chooses to practice, the holiday involves honoring death—of the living, of the old year, and of parts of ourselves we need to let go. Those parts, like ghosts, can shock or surprise us, particularly in the manner that they appear.

That year, my tiny apartment was a temple. We symbolically descended into the underworld, meeting the goddess and receiving her blessings. At that time in my priestess journey, my measure of a ritual's success was in the visible prostrations of my guests. The more people who cried, the better the job I was doing. Under that rule, I did a spectacular job that night. My guests wept. Some wailed. Some were on their knees, pounding the ground. Others cackled, their bodies shaking with pent-up laughter and the spirit of the room. Lives were being changed. I could see it. Well, for most of the guests, anyway.

For the entire ritual, my date stood in the corner with his arms crossed, his brow furrowed. I tried to ignore his expression and focus on the ritual. But as the night went on, he only looked more annoyed. I became angry, and then furious. I'd shared something deep and meaningful to me, something I'd never shared with even members of my family, let alone an intimate partner, and there he was, judging it. While my coveners chanted, I rehashed every fight we'd ever had. I imagined him blogging about the strange cult his ex-girlfriend had created, maybe ending it with some grand cliché like "Dodged a bullet there, friends!" As we released the goddess and the beloved dead, my other guests hugging and drying their tears, I stewed in my resentment. It had been a mistake to invite him. If Hekate is known for shaking the ghosts out of closets, she was clearly shaking one out of mine. Lesson learned. Thanks, Hekate.

But after everyone had gone, he asked me if we could step outside while he smoked. The night was loud and glowing with sounds and lights of New York City Halloween. We didn't speak. I was too angry, and he looked off at the cars and the people, silently smoking. I waited for him to condescend, and I practiced responses in my head, ready to defend myself and my coven, maybe even tell him to pack his bags and go home. If he was going to be judgmental, our weekend was clearly over.

But then he told me a story of a loss he'd suffered the year before. It wasn't the first time I'd heard the story, but in this telling I suddenly understood just how deeply the loss had affected him. It was then clear to me that he realized the same thing.

He lit a second cigarette and gestured to my apartment with it. "Something happened in there."

He had tucked his sorrow away, but he needed to mourn. Hekate had showed it to him, there in my living room, right before my critical, blind eyes.

I was suddenly and deeply ashamed. I had assumed he had been judging me, when in reality the judgmental one was me. Perhaps I'd let the past inform the present, ancient arguments and assumptions shaping my perspective, because his reaction to the ritual wasn't what I thought it should have been. All the while, this man standing quietly and stoically in the corner, who had always described himself as something between atheist and agnostic, was having a truly profound experience.

Hekate had indeed brought out ghosts of the past, but not in a way I'd expected. She brought out my dusty, moldy old judgments and broke my barometer of how magick "should" affect others. Sometimes, the greatest changes aren't visible to anyone but the person experiencing them. That night taught me that when I assume someone else is being critical of me, I should stop and ensure it isn't me tearing my own self down, which is often the true face of the judgment we assume we're receiving.

Hekate is a goddess of things that others fear, misunderstand, or even cast out of the mainstream world. She shows us comfort in the darkness. She shines a light on the places we need to heal. She can also show us the depths of our wickedness, highlighting our own powers to hurt or destroy. She reminds us of the spirits who have gone before us, connecting us to the lessons they leave behind. She reminds us of the magick in our blood. And just as the moon shines light into darkness, Hekate shines light into what within us is powerful and loving, forgiving and gracious. As we go through these lives of ours, there are moments when our own blessings, incredible qualities that could shake the earth and renew it whole, get lost in a period of darkness too. They become our own ghosts, haunting us, and often we fear and flee from them. But these are all Hekate's domain, and just as the ancient Greeks asked her to release the spirits to help them with their own magickal endeavors, we too can ask her to release the spirits to help us.

WORKING WITH HEKATE AND HER GHOSTS

There is no working with Hekate without working with the dead, and this is undoubtedly one of Hekate's most powerful guises. It's possible that the historical nature of the Hekatean spellwork with the dead is something many today might consider vile. But we must remember the context of these things. It was a different time, place, and people. We can learn from history without feeling the need to replicate or disparage it.

Some of this work, particularly spellwork in cemeteries, requires a great amount of care and conscientiousness. If you do decide to do magick work in a cemetery, be sure to check your local laws and the individual cemetery's rules. Hekatean work with the dead requires offerings, but not all offerings are appropriate for every cemetery. Second, we must offer respect for the living as much as the dead.

While cemeteries hold the remains of the departed, their service is really to the surviving loved ones, providing a place for them to mourn their losses. A modern Witch's need for privacy and secrecy may be less about "being caught" and more about not disturbing those in mourning.

Likewise, what is a Witch without the employ of ghosts and spirits? While today few of us have access or ability to tend the graves of our beloved dead, we can keep altars in our homes with candles, photographs, and other trinkets that connect us to our dead. In any culture around the world, Witchcraft is consistently linked to honoring and connecting with the dead, particularly dead ancestors. This may be as simple as leaving a cup of tea or coffee in the morning for your departed (which is something my husband and I do regularly), lighting candles for them, and saying their names aloud periodically. When it comes time for needing protection or assistance, if they have been appeased they are likely to help you with your endeavor.

With these things in mind, before doing any work in the cemetery, begin by forging a relationship both with the space and with the spirits resting there. Ideally, you'd do your work in a cemetery in which you have friends or relatives laid to rest. But working with the dead does not always require a cemetery. If you cannot visit the graves of your departed, or if they were cremated and do not have a burial site, consider building an altar to your beloved dead in your home. My husband and I have a shelf on our living room wall dedicated to our departed family members and friends. Lighting a candle on the altar is a good way to make an offering to the ancestors. It will also let them know when you want their attention.

If possible, these altars are best kept in the center of the home so that they can be surrounded by warmth and living energy, and perhaps so that they can "see" what's going on with their living loved ones. It's good to periodically offer other refreshments, such as a cup of coffee or tea, or a glass of wine or liquor. Some people offer tobacco if their beloved dead smoked when they were alive. Many traditions embrace this, but I believe the choice is a personal one. One Witch friend of mine used to offer liquor and cigarettes to her beloved dead. As she said, "They always came through and brought me whatever I wanted"; but she also felt a bit stuck. It wasn't until she stopped offering the substances that had killed her beloveds that her own life flourished. I try to strike a balance. I typically offer coffee or tea to my beloved dead, but on special occasions, such as a holiday, I might indulge them a little more.

I personally do not often work in cemeteries. I know I would be upset if I were visiting my grandfather's grave and discovered that a stranger had buried a spell in it. Then again, plenty of traditions use the graves of strangers for Witchcraft. It's not my place to say that it, as a general practice, is wrong.

If you feel called to use a graveyard (say, if you are not able to keep a shrine in your home and you cannot access any graveyards where you know anyone buried there), consider using an older cemetery, perhaps one that isn't regularly tended. When I was a little girl, I used to beg my mom to take my sister and me to a very old cemetery near the pool where we swam on summer afternoons. The graves were all well over a hundred years old and had largely been abandoned. Weeds grew up between the stones, and the names were largely faded and illegible. The dead were crying out for attention. If I feel the need to do cemetery work in the future, this is where I will do it.

If using such a cemetery, avoid making your first visit the one in which you ask for help with a spell. Begin by forming a relationship with the dead who are there. Clean up the graves—weed the grounds, clean the tombstones. Take care not to walk directly on older graves—one, out of respect, and two, to avoid them collapsing.

Bring fresh flowers. Talk to the dead. Sing to them. If their names are visible, say them aloud. If any religious symbols suggest their religion in life, try offering a prayer from their faith. Even if you do not know or practice their faith, most souls would gladly accept any well-intentioned prayer said in the tongue of the living.

When leaving the cemetery, take care not to bring any curious or bored spirits home with you. A few techniques performed in folk magick suggest the following:

- After leaving the cemetery, turn left in a circle three times and stamp your left foot.

- Make three stops on the way home (e.g., the gas station, the grocery store, the coffee shop).

- Take a path that crosses over a creek, river, or other water source.

- Before entering your home, tap and brush your shoulders to let the spirits know they cannot "ride" you into your home.

Then, when you absolutely need this help, make sure to bring an offering that would be pleasing to the spirits (tobacco, water, sweets, flowers, etc.). Make sure that everything you leave is biodegradable and nontoxic to animals. Spirits wouldn't appreciate plastic, Styrofoam, or items that don't break down quickly or end up choking our water system. The same should go for your actual spell materials. If you are writing down your spells, be sure to use natural paper that will break down easily.

As you work with the spirit for their assistance, be sure to continue to feed their grave regularly. When the spell has come to manifest, it's important to remind the spirit that their work is done and they can now return to resting. That may involve visiting their grave and inviting them to return, even singing them back to sleep so that they will not become lost or confused.

WORKING WITH HEKATE AND THE DEAD

Working with Hekate and the dead can be helpful. Think of it like Hekate vetting the applicants for the magickal job you want to do. She is aware of your needs and can help select the right helpful dead who can do the job you're looking to do. Be sure to make an offering to Hekate before and after inviting the dead to work with you.

If you use a tool, such as a wand or athame, this may be a time to bring it into the picture. If you do not use such tools, you can use your finger.

With a tool or your finger, draw a circle on the ground near your altar or near the grave of the soul you want to work with. Then draw a gateway, saying the following words aloud:

Hekate, guardian and gatekeeper,
I invite thee, I invoke thee, I seek thee;
Open the gates and allow the spirits to come through.
Protect me from baneful spirits,
Bring only those who desire to help.
I offer [offerings]; in return I seek [what you need help with].

A Ritual to Release a Symbolic Ghost

Sometimes, experiences or memories of living people can haunt us. We struggle to stop focusing on them and find ourselves replaying old conversations in our heads. These are symbolic ghosts. While they are not actual spirits pestering us, they can disturb us all the same.

While working on this chapter, I had a recurring dream of someone from my past. We'd ended our friendship on quite painful terms many years before. Reaching out to apologize was not an option, so I found myself often speaking to them in my head, saying I was sorry for my part in things even though I was not solely at fault. In the dream, which I'd had for years, we stood in the same room but ignored each other as hard as we could. I meditated with Hekate to ask why I kept dreaming about this person and saw a vision of the following spell. While I didn't know what it was meant to do when I began, before I completed the rite I realized that my continuously apologizing was keeping us energetically linked, preventing us both from moving forward with our lives. The next night, I had a dream of saying goodbye to this person and walking away.

To start the spell, first find an image representing the person or situation. If you don't have such a thing, using a Tarot card that depicts two people is helpful. Write your initials beneath the image of one person, and the initials of the other person or the situation on the other. Alternatively, use a face card from a deck of playing cards. Write your and the other party's or situation's initials beneath one side of each face.

Using a dab of spicy oil (hot pepper oil is good, or a regular hot sauce like Sriracha), anoint each face of the image or playing card. Wash your hands immediately afterward.

Cut the two faces apart, declaring yourself free from the situation.

Outside or in a well-ventilated area, burn the card. As the smoke rises, declare that the bonds have been severed. If you cannot burn the cards, a smushing ritual, in which you dissolve the card in salty water, is also effective. (For more on smushing rituals, see *Water Witchcraft* by Annwyn Avalon.)

Scatter the ashes or water on a crossroads, leaving or performing an offering to Hekate and any spirits who want to consume the energetic remains of the work you've performed.

CHAPTER SIX

The Dangerous Goddess and the Dangerous Witch

Hekate isn't a savior. She isn't going to come down, fix everything, and pull you out of the muck. She'll give you the rope, the shovel, the keys or the torch, and she'll expect you to pull yourself up and out. She isn't a mother in the cookies-and-milk sense. She isn't going to kiss your boo-boos and make it all better. She's more composed than that—and she expects you to be as well. Hekate is a witch because she's resourceful. She is the person who is leading the march for women's equality; she is the librarian who is able to find you just the right book with only a color and a vague title. She is the friend who says, "Don't worry, sit down, drink some water/wine, I got this." She's the person who keeps a cool head in a crisis. She does the work because it needs to be done, not to get accolades. Hekate has had a hand in my life since before I knew it. Most of the time, her signs and nudges are subtle—not blatant. They require you to look a bit deeper. She isn't one to shout.

—Sarah Bitner, modern priestess of Hekate

The path of the Witch is dangerous. These dangers might be symbolic, pushing us to embrace and accept parts of ourselves we'd rather keep hidden. Sometimes, however, they manifest in the strange situations that appear as we walk this path. When I lived in New York, I walked into such a situation while doing some work for Hekate. I was coming home from the post office, where I'd mailed a donation of books to a friend and priestess of Hekate who was building a library for incarcerated Pagans. When I arrived at my building, a young woman leaned out the front door, shouting at a man as he ran down the stairs, her purse under his arm, and raced away. I had never met this woman before, but she threw herself into my arms, crying. When the police arrived, I jumped into the cruiser with her, which took us to identify the man, who had been caught about six blocks away.

While I sat with her at the police station, I wondered if Hekate actually sent me, or if I was just in the right place at the wrong time. I wondered if I had helped or just gotten tripped up with something that wasn't my business. On the day I went to court, the prosecuting attorney was a very pregnant young woman with a Greek surname. It was a sign to me that Hekate had certainly been present throughout the entire experience.

Today, many people's idea of a goddess is generally kind and good, but perhaps misunderstood by the patriarchy. The idea of the goddess being cruel, monstrous, or otherwise is often blamed on more mainstream religions; many modern Witches and Pagans believe that these faiths have demonized feminine deities. In some cases, that's true—but not always. Most pre-Christian deities, including Hekate, did have terrifying shadow selves. Like humans, they were good most of the time; but when they were bad, they were horrid. The dagger, one of Hekate's symbols, may have referred to her ability to cut a soul loose from this life to pass into the realm of

Hades, or cut the umbilical cord to let a new life into this world. It's also thought to have represented the culling of herbs. Those herbs were often meant to heal, but in in some of her myths these herbs were poisonous and the dagger may have symbolized a more sinister use.

The occultist Aleister Crowley wrote in his 1929 book *Moonchild* that Hekate is "a thing altogether of Hell; barren, hideous, and malicious, the queen of death and evil witchcraft. Hekate is the crone, the woman past all hope of motherhood, her soul black with envy and hatred of happier mortals."[1] In this, he describes Hekate as both the holder and harbinger of humankind's potential for wickedness. It is this wicked potential that has often been imposed on Witches, who have historically been blamed for tragedies or other phenomena (natural or unnatural) that defied general understanding at the time.

But since the end of the twentieth century, there has been a concerted effort to change the conversation around what it means to be a Witch. Today, a Witch can mean being an ecological conservationist, a healer, a feminist, a warrior, or a rebel. It often involves accepting the divine as at least partially feminine, or no gender at all. For quite a while, most Wiccans (many of whom self-identified as Witches) rejected anything considered baneful or wicked. But Hekate, a quintessential Witch for millennia, has had a reputation of being both a benevolent goddess of power and healing as well as something more sinister. It is said that she was the first to observe the strength of aconite, a poisonous plant of the buttercup family, and to discover the aromatic verbena among the poisonous herbs, and was sometimes rumored to test them on unsuspecting people.[2] This doesn't mean that Hekate is a bad goddess, or shouldn't be honored in modern Witchcraft. Again, we must remember that the scarier guises of ancient deities reflect the experiences of the people at the time. To ignore these details or gloss over them would undermine the history of these great beings. No matter how a modern Witch categorizes Hekate, baneful or beneficent, one consistent truth is that she is a *dangerous* goddess.

Nowhere is Hekate's identity as a dangerous goddess more prevalent than in the myths of Medea. Because of certain horrifying elements in Medea's story, she is frequently ignored in contemporary Witchcraft practice, relegated as being one of the great villains of ancient mythology—the archetypal crazy woman, so rattled with rage and jealousy that she takes the lives of her two children. Her name was frequently invoked by ancient Witches using potions to thwart enemies, to take revenge, usually while invoking Hekate.[3]

Described as semidivine, Medea was sometimes said to be a daughter of Hekate, but the terms daughter and priestess were interchangeable in some traditions or translations. Through Hekate, Medea learned the use of magickal herbs, including those for healing, medicinal, and culinary properties, not just the use of deadly plants.[4] Medea is often held up as the archetype of a bad Witch, but when looking deeper into Medea's story we learn that the terrible acts are less about character and are more reactions to extreme circumstances. We also learn a few more things about Hekate.

In the Greek epic the *Argonautica*, Medea is first introduced as a dedicated priestess and dutiful family member. She falls in love with Jason of the Argonauts, the leader of a band of sea-roaming heroes. Zeus's jealous wife Hera, for her own reasons, designed a plan to make Medea fall in love with Jason by having Eros (known for creating mismatched couples), strike her with an arrow. In other stories, Aphrodite gave Jason a spell meant to seduce Medea, so that he could use her for her magickal powers.[5] It is this love that inspires Medea's plot against her father's ambitions. However, Medea is racked with guilt over her decision to choose Jason over her family.

Meanwhile, Jason has been tasked with taking the fleece of a golden ram, which he must do to take his seat as the rightful king of the city of Ioclus. This golden fleece is magickal and so heavily guarded that he requires magickal help. King Aeetes, Medea's father, offers to give Jason the fleece if he can complete three seemingly impossible tasks: yoke two fire-breathing oxen and plough a field with them, sow a field with the teeth of a dragon, and overcome the giant serpent that guards the fleece—one that never sleeps.

All the while, Medea hides in the shadows, watching from afar as her beloved is humiliated by her father. She worries for him, intensely, but as she sleeps that night, she realizes that the trick her father laid was only on Jason, and not on her. She decides to help him. At dawn, she visits a shrine to Hekate and summons her (as Brimo) seven times from the underworld to help her aid Jason. Later, when she meets with Jason, she offers him a charm she has had blessed by Hekate to help him with his endeavor. She also gives him pertinent information and potions he will need to succeed. And she instructs him to make a sacrifice to Hekate. Shortly thereafter, Jason petitions Hekate (as Brimo) with the sacrifice of a sheep in a predawn rite. She appears before him in a terrifying vision, frightening him so much that he steps back and nearly runs away. Hekate, as Brimo, appears alongside serpents twisting themselves among the surrounding oaks, with the sounds of the hounds of hell filling the air. He had a vision of "countless torches" and shrieking nymphs, and the ground shook where the goddess walked.[6] As terrified as he was, Jason returned to his comrades and did not look back.

Medea's gifts to Jason included an ointment that would protect him from the oxen's flames. She also warned him that when Jason sowed the dragon's teeth, they would turn into fierce warriors bent on killing him. Armed with this foreknowledge, he throws a boulder into the crowd, which causes the soldiers to turn on one another. Finally,

Medea and Jason together approach the great serpent guarding the coveted fleece. After calling upon Hekate for assistance, Medea sprinkles a potion made with juniper and other herbs from her magickal collection on the creature's eyes, causing it to sleep, and allowing Jason to take the fleece and for them to both escape to his ship.

As they flee, Medea makes a sacrifice to Hekate to help them hasten their escape. Yet her brother pursues her. She plots with Jason to kill him, which he does, dismembering and hiding the body so her father's men, in fear of being blamed for either the death or being unable to find the body, abandon their quest to retrieve Medea. Medea helps Jason's crew subdue other monsters and face other challenges along the way through her magick, including defeating the great Talos, a man of bronze who threatens to smash their ships with stones. Medea sang and prayed to petition assistance from the death spirits, along with the hounds of Hades, the otherworld, ultimately bewitching the great Talos and sending terrifying phantoms ahead of them to aid their escape.[7]

Medea began her story as a dutiful daughter, a priestess whose work involved healing. But because of Hera's interference and her own blinding passions for Jason, she turns her magick and cunning toward murder and destruction, all to support the man she loves.

Other tales of Medea give her a more nuanced and sympathetic story.[8] In one, Hekate is Medea's mother, described as more queen than goddess, brazenly lawless, fond of the hunt; but when her luck failed, she turned her bow on men. Medea was also listed as a keen contriver of mixtures of deadly drugs (called *pharmaka*) and credited with the discovery of aconite. Hekate destroyed her father (who was the Titan god Perses in this story) and took over the throne, building a temple to Artemis. In this version, Medea learns the powers of plants from Hekate, but her own inclination was to save strangers, rather than expose them to danger. When her father learns of

Medea's efforts to rescue strangers whom he would also put to death, he plots to have her killed. Medea flees and hides in the precinct of Helios, where Jason and the Argonauts find her wandering on the shore. Finding sympathy with her plight, they offer her their protection, and Medea in return promises to help them until they complete their proposed contest. Jason swears an oath that he will marry and care for her his whole life.

In this version, Medea's gifts are equally as crucial in the Argonauts' quest. She charms the gates of the cities to open, an ability only a princess could offer, which allows the Argonauts to enter and sack the city. She offers to kill the false king Pelias, who had stolen the throne that was Jason's birthright, via her own magickal abilities. She had never caused murder with her own potions, but she agrees to do so in order to punish those deserving of punishment. Through magickal disguise and strategizing with the invading Argonauts, she tricks Pelias's own daughters to kill him themselves.

Jason and Medea wed and live together for ten years. He was said to revere her for not only her beauty but also her self-restraint and other virtues. But as she ages, Jason becomes attracted to a younger woman and attempts to divorce Medea. She refuses to comply with the divorce, loathe to accept the humiliation of being left for another woman, but also loathe to break the vows she made before her gods. Jason withdraws from the marriage anyway and plans to marry the younger woman. In the aftermath, Medea calls upon Hekate to fulfill a murderous vow, summoning a vision of Hekate that includes snakes in her hair and bloody hands clutching a torch, begging her to exhibit the most terrifying version of herself and bring death upon her ex-husband's new wife and her father, and other royals associated with them. She then wishes for something she believes is even harsher for her ex-husband: that he live but be destined to wander strange cities, destitute.[9]

Some stories say that Medea disguises herself and enters the palace, setting it afire. Jason survives, but his bride and her father do not. Other stories say that Medea smears the wedding gifts with poison, which kills the young bride. In the story of the fire, Medea was so enraged that Jason survived that she kills the children she bore to him. In some translations, she believes she would make the children immortal through this act but fails. The children are sometimes said to have become part of the *biaiothanatoi*, angry souls who were dangerous and needed to be appeased, which would also make them part of Hekate's domain.[10] Jason, in grief and shame from the loss of his children and his new wife, takes his own life while Medea flees.

Medea gave up her family, her home, her comforts, and more, and dedicated her life to be a wife to Jason and the mother of his children. Through the gifts she gave him, he excelled, reveling in glory and praise. She gave away all of herself to help her husband, and in doing so had no place to retreat to when he rejected her, as returning to her family would mean certain death. Then, Medea is often immortalized as a wicked Witch. Some of this is understandable, given her ultimate act of horror. But setting her specific actions aside, parts of Medea's story may provoke some empathy. How many of us have found ourselves making extraordinary sacrifices, only to feel that these acts are taken for granted? How many Witches have performed acts of magick for others, only to find that our gifts are mocked, devalued, or not reciprocated?

It is tempting to look at Medea's story and receive it as a warning of what *not* to do (either become involved with someone like Medea, jealous and rageful, or someone like Jason, who needs to absorb the talents and abilities of others to be successful). But it's not all bad for Medea in the end. In some tellings, she was said to go on to heal the hero Hercules, remarry two other times and give birth to more children who would become kings. Although the gods were horrified that Medea murdered her children, the universal order takes some pity on her, perhaps through recognizing Jason's painful actions, too.

Witches are emotional creatures. We feel joy and sorrow deeply. Betrayal breaks our hearts in a hard way, and the bridges we burn flare hot. We can love and care for people with a poignant intensity. We can also hurt, whether we mean to or not. We love hard and mourn our losses for a long time. Even if we never act on our worst impulses, effective Witches are aware of their individual capacity to harm. Most of us turn to Witchcraft because we, like Medea, experienced deep hurt or harm along our journeys. Witchcraft is a way to give power back to the disempowered, or reconnect with that power when it is taken from us.

But it is easy, and sometimes tempting, to misuse our gifts. Particularly when we are new to the work, the most powerful spells become like shiny toys in our hands. We *can* use them. So why not? Christopher Penczak sums this up perfectly in his book *The Mighty Dead*:

> Any of us who have gained any magickal power have come into positions when we have wanted to, or indeed have, abused it. We have acted with less than impeccable motives. An insult, a loss of something we wanted, an argument can all lead us to directing our power in little, and big ways, against those we perceive are our enemies. The more personally affronted by their actions and the need for retaliation, the less justified we are in taking that action. I have no problem with defensive or even offensive magick when necessary, but like the honorable martial artist, I believe you use only the necessary force to neutralize the situation. But with psychic power and spellcraft, it is easy to let passions carry us and

go overboard, with far more than what is necessary in that situation.

I'll admit it. I've been there. I've cast harsh, baneful spells when my feelings were hurt or my ego was bruised. And when my feelings cooled and sufficient time passed, I saw how unnecessary my reactions were. My anger may have been justified, but reacting magickally to something that could have been resolved through a conversation or simply distance from the situation has left me cleaning up the mess years later. Our spells don't end when the candle goes out. The anger I've sent out in the form of a spell because I felt disrespected has sometimes taken on a life of its own. All human emotions can take the form of spiritual beings. A home full of love and joy can laugh on its own. A space containing a trauma may replay the trauma, in the form of a haunting, the terrible energy of the act repeating over and over like a song stuck on repeat for those sensitive enough to feel it. Likewise, anger can create its own forms that can run rampant in the spiritual fabric that connects us all, doing damage for years after we've moved on from the situation that prompted us to create them in the first place.

This does not mean that our anger is never justified. It doesn't mean that we shouldn't get angry. And it doesn't mean that we should never use our magick against those who have harmed us. Particularly if the harm done to us is likely to be done against someone else, using magick to prevent someone who caused harm from doing so again can be a moral imperative. We should ask ourselves, with the power of magick at our disposal, shouldn't we maximize its use? Does it make sense to use our abilities to attack someone over an issue that has little impact on the overall arc of humanity, or perhaps save that energy for larger things that do? Sometimes, these moments of fury can help us do great work. In that way, Witches are wonderfully dangerous. It is up to us individually to determine the best use of such potent energy and powerful potential.

THE DANGEROUS WITCH

The current world is full of things to be angry about: severe economic inequality; violence against people because of their gender identity, race, or religion; environmental destruction; and more. Today, many Witches use their powers to address these things—and they work. Before same-sex marriage was legal in the United States, my coven organized a major ritual to help legalize it in New York State. At that time, the measure was in the hands of the New York State Senate. We created a great ball of energy designed to break blockages and allow marriage for all in our state, and we directed it toward an image of the state senate's seal. Six weeks later, the ban on same-sex marriage was overturned. While we certainly weren't the sole source of the change (activists and organizers had been working on this issue for well over a decade and are rightfully owed the credit for the success), I believe we helped provide a boost the effort needed at that time.

Sometimes, when I've been especially angry, the anger seemed to only stoke more anger, with no proper resolution. This isn't to say my anger wasn't justified. In many situations, it was very much justified. But as a more seasoned Witch, I've learned that retaliation doesn't undo what has been done to me. But there are plenty of things in my country that deserved great anger. Instead of shaping the anger into a spell to return a bruised ego or hurt feelings, I often shape my anger to address the origins of systemic oppression. Likewise, the more that I learned about Hekate, the more I was unsurprised that Hekate, and her Witches, have a long history of establishing order fighting injustice, making them dangerous to those who break laws or threaten others.

In several Greek papyri (writings containing magickal spells, hymns, and rituals from ancient Greece and Rome), Hekate was invoked as part of a triad of Hekate-Selene-Artemis. According to the writer Hesiod, Hekate's functions included law.[11] On one picture from a *lekythos* (an ancient Greek vessel used for storing oils), Hekate appears to use her dogs to punish humans for their wrongdoings in the upper world—dogs drinking the blood of the guilty for impiety to the gods or injustice to men or other crimes.[12] While Hekate isn't often listed as a judge of human righteousness or guilt, she does seem to dole out justice when it's called for. Ancient Witches may have invoked her for that very reason.

One curse tablet contains a spell either on behalf of a victim who had been slandered by someone else or against someone who shared the mysteries of a Hekatean cult, a presumably grave error among the cult's initiates.[13] The caster asked the Hekate triune to "take away her sleep and give her punishment in her mind, and burning in her soul," for defiling the mysteries or for spreading slanderous gossip. This particular spell required goat's fat, blood and filth, the menstrual flow of a dead virgin, the heart of one untimely dead, and the "magickal material" of a dead dog and a woman's embryo (although the specifics of this magickal material are not obvious), and the sacrifice of a sea falcon, a vulture, and a mouse.

In another spell, an inscription calls on Hekate to avenge those who urinate in, and therefore pollute, the eastern passage of a southern gate at Ephesus, an ancient Greek city and a place of frequent commerce, the ruins of which are located along the coast of present-day Turkey, and where she was also seen as a guardian of the crossroads. It's likely that it was believed that pollution in this area could bring foul conditions to the overall city, and therefore Hekate was invoked to bring swift justice on those who committed such an act. After their executions, when bodies of murderers were taken to crossroads, a gathered crowd would throw stones at the corpses as a method of purifying the city. A corpse would be left there unburied, perhaps to let Hekate decide what should happen to their soul. On one black-figured lekythos, two female figures to the right and left of Hekate appear to give orders for the soul to be punished. One, or both, of these characters might be the Erinyes, who lived in the underworld and punished perjurers and matricides.[14]

THE WITCH, THE REBEL

Some stories paint Medea as a rebellious woman whose refusal to conform to what is expected of her threatens the social order. In one folk song, Medea (here called Aletis) spent her life wandering in exile from one city-state to another because she rejected the standard female roles of dutiful daughter, submissive wife, and nurturing mother.[15] Other descriptions of Medea show her as a vessel of both great power and danger through her intelligence, skills, and power:

> It is not because of her beauty or her good deeds that you find Medea pleasing, but she knows incantations and she culls dreadful plants with her enchanted sickle. She works hard to draw the struggling moon down from its path and to bury the horses of the sun in darkness. She reins back waters and brings rivers to a halt in their descent. She transports woods and rocks, as if alive, from their place. She wanders amid tombs, ungirt, her hair in disarray, and gathers the pick of the bones from warm pyres. She places binding spells on people from afar . . . and she does other things it would have been better . . . not to know.[16]

Whether one could argue that Medea is evil or not, it cannot be disputed that she is indeed dangerous. She cannot be controlled; she does not abide by rules she does not respect. In many cases, her potential to be dangerous comes from the lessons learned and invoked from Hekate. Fueled by the pain that only a person wronged can experience, and armed with the powerful weapons of Witchcraft, Medea becomes an embodiment of the dangerous goddess and Witch.

One of Medea's dangers was not what she did or what she was capable of, but what she knew. Witches embrace the things that scare others, be they spirits of the dead or the use of plants in spells. We know the secrets of making changes to the world around us, and those things can drive people away from us. We become the keeper of secrets, whether we are doing a Tarot reading for another person or listening to someone share their psychic or spiritual experiences. But to some, simply by knowing that we hold this knowledge, we may be perceived as dangerous. Witchcraft, and goddesses such as Hekate, lead us to revel in the things about us that make us different. It allows us to dance down the paths that others have felt too much shame to trod. It encourages us to hold, kiss, and become one with the parts of ourselves that others are afraid to embrace in themselves. We expose the false rules that others hold so fiercely. This may make us a danger to the status quo.

At the same time, Medea's story is a lesson in boundaries. Most Witches have had one, or more, of the following experiences: the religious conservative person scolding the Witch for their practices, only to ask for a Tarot reading in the next breath; the well-meaning but ignorant friend who, usually after a few drinks, will say that they shouldn't be the Witch's friend because their religion or culture says that Witches are inherently evil, only to then brag to their other friends about knowing a Witch; the relative who begs the Witch to give up Witchcraft and go to church, but then begs for a love spell to make their ex return. It hurts. It harms. Still, many Witches feel that they should be available and willing to give of their gifts, even to those who harm them. Hey, Witchy friend: I'm here to tell you that you don't have to give your magick away, prove your power, or give any time to people who harm you. Let us learn from Medea and not be beholden to work for others simply because we can. It's OK to say no. It's fine to let people face their own journeys, to acquire their own golden fleeces without us—particularly if they don't show us the courtesy we deserve.

Witchcraft on its own isn't evil, but it can push the most extreme parts of ourselves into the light. The pharmaka can either help or heal depending on their use. This is neither bad or good, but it is definitely dangerous. A dog, even a fluffy little one, can be a danger in a specific context, but also a comfort or protector. The Witch can also be dangerous. But let us be dangerous in the right context— doing so with intention. We can choose to be like Medea, to let these extreme parts of self consume us, or pivot to use our tools to defeat an oppressor. No one can tell us exactly when or how to best use our dangerous selves but us. We are going to make mistakes. We may act too harshly in a situation and need to rectify our decision. We may not act and later wish we had. Rarely do Witches look back and feel completely confident that they did everything perfectly. Fortunately, Witchcraft isn't about perfection. It is messy and often confusing. We do the best we can, learn from it, and try again.

Prayer to the Dangerous Goddess

This prayer can be helpful if you're feeling angry and are looking for a way to use your magick in a helpful way. It can also be used to figure out how you yourself are a dangerous Witch, and better understand how to use those tools. Say the prayer aloud in the presence of your altar, at an outdoor space you feel is attuned to Hekate, or anytime you want to connect with this part of self.

Hekate, Brimo, underworld Witch,
I embrace my dagger; show me where to cut.
For the greatest good, the most powerful end,

May I be righteous in my actions,
May any harm be justified and serve the highest good.
Raise your torch, and show me the way.
The dark mother, the queen, the just goddess,
Lead me to swift and right action.

Spell to Bind an Oppressive Force

When you are dealing with an oppressive force, either against your-self personally or in a community or country, get a candle. The color isn't important, but white or black tends to have the best results.

Carve the name of the person or entity causing the oppression into the candle. Then take the candle in your palms and channel all angry thoughts pertaining to the situation into it.

Say the following aloud:

As they have done unto me, now have Hekate do unto them.
Let the weak be strong, and the unjust receive their due.
By Hekate, Selene, Artemis,
So mote it be.

Burn the candle all the way down. Wrap the cooled remaining wax in twine nine times and bury it in a place you walk over fre-quently (such as under or near the front step of your house or build-ing), so you are "stepping" on the oppression whenever you walk by.

Ritual for Inner Peace

If you feel your anger is not serving you, perhaps making you bitter and occupying more space in your head than you would like, and you are looking for a sense of peace, take a knife, athame, or other blade you use for ritual or magick and bring it to your space of ritual. You could even use a pair of scissors or a butter knife—but don't use one that you then plan to include with the rest of your regular kitchen utensils or office supplies. Secondhand or thrift stores can provide some very inexpensive, interesting options for this tool.

In your sacred space, envision the source of your anger in front of you. Then envision a chain connecting you to this vision. Most people see these chains as being connected to their heart, forehead, stomach, or groin area. You might find yourself seeing more than one. When I've been *really* angry, I've seen them in all four places!

While understanding that you are not being required to pardon anyone for their actions, unless this is what you feel is right for you, you are severing yourself from the situation so that you can find peace and renewal. Say the following:

With the blade of Brimo, I release myself from bondage to you.

With the blade, slice the air in front of the space(s) where you envisioned the chain. Perform this incantation three times in each area.

If you are not already at a physical crossroads when you are done with this work, take the blade to the crossroads and slap it on the ground three times, giving thanks to Hekate for helping you make this rite.

You may find that you'll need to do this ritual several times over the coming days and weeks. It's very tempting to return to that connective anger. I've sometimes had to repeat it years later when another situation triggers those same feelings.

If it doesn't already have other purposes, the blade can be used in protective or justice work in the future. It can also be a great tool for doing the cutting spell described in the previous chapter.

CHAPTER SEVEN

Keeper of the Keys

And the Titanian goddess, the moon, rising from a far land, beheld her [Medea] as she fled distraught, and fiercely exulted over her, and thus spake to her own heart: "Not I alone then stray to the Latinian cave, nor do I alone burn with love for fair Endymion; oft times with thoughts of love have I been driven away by thy crafty spells, in order that in the darkness of night thou mightest work thy sorcery at ease, even the deeds dear to thee."
—Apollonius Rhodius, *Argonautica*[1]

When I was six years old, our family moved from Tennessee to Oregon. I missed my friends and old school terribly. I believed that someday I would find a magickal key, and when I found that key a door would appear in my closet. The Key to Tennessee would allow me to walk through this portal and see my friends whenever I wanted. I even asked for it in a letter to Santa. It remains a family legend.

Later that year, while visiting family in California, my sister and I found an orphaned key in our grandmother's junk drawer, marked "T." It had to be the key to Tennessee. What else could it be? We were ecstatic. A ten-hour drive is hard on small children, but it is *excruciating* for small children who believe they have a magickal key in their hands and a portal waiting for them at home. When we got home, we raced upstairs to my bedroom. I probably don't have to describe the sickening disappointment when we flung open the closet door, only to find no portal in the wall. My sister tried to unlock the air, in case the door was invisible. It wasn't. We looked in every other closet in the house, but we could not find the door to Tennessee.

What may be surprising was that I didn't lose faith in magick that day. Rather, that bitter disappointment actually made a Witch of me. What I didn't know was that by believing in that little key, I was taking part in an ancient tradition of bestowing magick to keys. Keys are a small and commonplace item, but they are integral to living. They open doors; they keep intruders out. A locked door can be a powerfully frustrating object (says the author, who has locked herself out of her house an embarrassing number of times). But a locked drawer or box can hold treasures and mystery. When I gave my nephew a journal for his birthday, he was most excited by the lock and key, which could keep his mystery. Many of humanity's inventions have become obsolete over several millennia, but until very recently (with the invention of key cards) keys largely remained the same. Practically, they help us protect ourselves. Symbolically, they link us to the past, being as important now as they were then. Spiritually, they represent the unlocking of mysteries.

The key, being one of Hekate's most poignant symbols, represents mystery, along with the unlocking of secrets or keeping them hidden away. Hekate's keys also represent the mysteries of the cosmos, death, and spiritual virtues. She is called Kleidoukhos: the keeper of the keys. It is perhaps through this important symbol of Hekate that we can grasp the use of magick and better understand it.

HEKATE: KEY KEEPER

Keys appear in the hands of many Hekate figures. These keys represent several different things, some of which are quite practical. Early inscriptions call her a protector of entrances, which the key image may represent. In ancient Greece, shrines of Hekate were commonly found on doorsteps. As the protector of entrances and other liminal places, both public and private, she defended people against lurking spirits. The physical area before the gates of the temple, city, or house was sacred to Hekate. Her keys may have represented not only her protection of these spaces but also protection of whole cities. Hekate could close the city against all dangers or open it to benign influences, both of which were part of her role as a protector of thresholds and gateways.[2] In one appearance, Hekate refers to herself as "a goddess in full armor and with weapons," which may have been meant to ward off threatening demons from someone working magick.[3] All of these roles are easily symbolized by the familiar key image in Hekate iconography, but this last example may also symbolize that Hekate the key keeper was a friend to Witches in particular.

The key may be a very ancient part of Hekate's image. Her role as a goddess of passage and liminal points can be traced back to her worship in the Asia Minor, preceding her Greek worship.[4] It's possible that the key imagery was inherited from this ancient role. The key-keeper role may also suggest another practical role, that of the provider. In Bronze Age Greece (roughly 3000–1000 BCE), images of female key keepers seem to refer to a community support role. Temples served as not only places of worship but also communal food storage centers. Therefore, the key keeper provided both religious rites and food for the community—two crucial roles that afforded them enormous power, prestige, and possibly fear, as the person with this role should not be treated carelessly.[5] Hekate may have been a great key keeper: a protector of the people, as well as one who could encourage a bountiful harvest . . . or withhold it.

A grand rite dedicated to Hekate was known as the Procession of the Key, which was a major element in a larger festival called Hekatesia. This procession was likely linked with a native, ancient, and non-Greek custom.[6] According to a description in the Lagina temple in Asia minor, eunuch priests and a priestess carrying a key led the procession. Some writings suggest that the key-holder role was a position of great honor, most often filled by a daughter of a priest of Hekate.[7] Although the function and purpose of this festival and procession are unknown, they are believed to have had a chthonic nature. Hekate's key likely represented her role in the underworld.[8] It's possible that these rites were in honor of the ancestors, but they also likely celebrated the death and regeneration of the earth as reflected through agricultural cycles. The two focus points were not terribly diverse. In such a worldview, life, death, and regeneration were closely aligned, the ancestors sharing the realm of the food source. The key and its rites protected the world from the influence of negative spirits, opened the realms for new children to be born, and embodied the fertility of the land. The key, while considered to be the symbol of the goddess, was also a symbol of male fertility.[9]

This and perhaps other rites involving Hekate's keys may have represented purification, either for those who participated in the rites or for purifying the land. Rituals honoring transitions in ancient Greece and ancient Rome began with the removal of pollution, meaning that entrances would also come to be associated with purification rites.[10] Gates and doorways of temples marked the boundaries between sacred and non-sacred space, private and public, clean and polluted. Crossing such a boundary might have required a ritual of purification. In some cases, setting an image of Hekate near a threshold helped in this purification, as it was believed she had a special interest in and control over such thresholds.[11] The act of passing through a gateway was itself a purification rite. Hekate's keys, as connected to this threshold of purification, may have had a role in removing both spiritual and physical impurities.

Hekate's key symbolism was not only about physical protection or agricultural production. She held a role as both the gate and key keeper of the underworld, and was the one who could open the realms between the living and the dead. One of Hekate's titles was "living one [who has the] keys of Death and Hades."[12] When the Trojan hero Aeneas attempts to enter the underworld, he invokes Hekate for her aid in bridging the realms of the living and the dead.[13] Her keys were sometimes called "the badge of Hades," specifically meant to open the gates of the underworld, a role that could be more sinister in nature.[14] As key keeper, Hekate could imprison mortal souls in Hades's frightening realm. In one underworld scene, Hekate is shown as a monstrous female figure with dogs, commanding presence over a small human figure, one stripped of all clothing and condemned to undergo a frightful punishment in Hades.[15] It's not clear whether she is a guide or a guard, or whether she is assisting or imprisoning the soul, but it may be safely assumed that she embodied both roles.

As explored earlier in the chapter, Hekate the key keeper was important to Witches and other magick workers in the ancient world. Remembering that a Witch's magick frequently depended on assistance from the dead, Hekate's keys were crucial, as they opened not only the gates of Hades but also the gates to prophetic messages accessed by Sybil, an oracular priestess who could deliver the words of the gods to the living.[16] The key keeper was one aspect of Hekate that Witches could not live without.

Hekate's keys likely also symbolized transitions. Feasts to Hekate were sometimes held on the final day of each month, which was marked by the dark moon, before the first sliver of the new moon could be seen. This feast was called Deîpnon, and one of the things that it may have celebrated was the transition between the old month and the new. As a patroness of young girls, especially during adolescence and puberty, Hekate guarded their transition to womanhood and eventual marriage. In some stories, she was also known as the nursing mother, unlocking the passage between womb and life.[17] The keys may have represented Hekate's guardianship of these pivotal points of life.

Hekate's keys generally reflected common areas of the lives of the ancients: protection of the home, access to food, natural rites of passage, even contact with the dead, which was a regular part of life. But just as a key may be taken for granted until it's lost and a door cannot be opened, Hekate's keys may also represent facets of life that aren't given much thought daily, but whose disruption is felt very deeply. Even so, Hekate and her keys had other and arguably greater significance.

OPENING THE DOOR TO GREATER UNDERSTANDING

Hekate's keys also represent her role as gatekeeper to the greater mysteries of the cosmos, including humanity's overall purpose. This role is reflected in the *Chaldean Oracles*, a set of spiritual texts used by philosophers in the years 300–600 CE, which were said to have been dictated to mortal writers directly from Hekate and Apollo (possibly meant to represent the moon and the sun, or a great divine spirit of the universe). They originated as a poem of which, sadly, only fragments are preserved. In their time, they were used as proof of the will of the gods.[18] They stemmed from the belief in which the world is a foul tomb, but through the oracles' practices, one could transcend their "foul" form and become one with the cosmic soul. Also called the world soul, this great power source was believed to provide a standard for correct, harmonious order, a divine and eternal source of rational life, and the crowning creation of all intelligible and eternal entities endowed with reason and harmony.[19] Basically, it is the best of all of us; the best we could ever be, in this life or in any after.

In addition to delivering information from these oracles to humanity, Hekate was also portrayed as an intermediary between the different realms.[20] As a great key holder, she was believed to close the boundaries of things within the cosmos, as she was bestowed with the ability to bind together and harmonize diverse elements.[21] Hekate guarded certain points of access to this great soul. The oracles describe something called "the Gulf of Hekate," as a point of passage in the journey to the cosmic soul. In this gulf, souls could dole out or receive punishment for crimes they committed as spirits, perhaps on command of Witches who summoned them to do their bidding; the special abilities and goodwill of this goddess were important for souls who were seeking salvation.[22]

Hekate's keys may have also represented the practices outlined in the oracles—practices that when embraced and executed could help a mortal soul elevate and find access to the cosmic soul. In the oracles, her keys represent the virtues of love and strength, two things known as Hekate's sacred fires.[23]

The idea of the cosmic soul has parallels in other religions, two examples being the Christian heaven and the nirvana of Buddhism. While there is no single conclusive belief among contemporary Witches concerning an afterlife, many believe that the soul continues after death, even if that afterlife is mysterious and unknowable. Most Witches seem comfortable with this unknowable aspect, accepting that is a great mystery we'll never fully understand. Many of us were

raised with religious backgrounds that preached an idea of a puni-
tive divine being, waiting to judge us as good or unworthy upon our
death. These judgments were usually based more on how we lived,
whom we loved, or how we indulged in pleasure, rather than whether
we were kind to others or not. This being would then give us access
to its own form of the cosmic soul, or banish us to its own form of
Hades (many might recognize this as the Christian hell). It's often
this belief that turns many Witches away from the religions of their
youth. There is an undeniable freedom in removing oneself from this
mindset, but it can also leave many Witches confused. We are no longer on a restrictive path, shaped by shame and control. Instead, we
are wandering through a wilderness, free of that judgment, but may
wonder if our wandering is aimless.

Hekate as the key keeper may provide a helpful middle path.
Though our current culture encourages us to be individualistic,
humans are innately pack animals. We crave a community. Perhaps there is a great desire to return to a communal soul, but not
if the path there means sacrificing vital parts of self. Also, because
we are community creatures, we may naturally fear rejection. This is
frightening enough when approaching a new community, but it can
be even more terrifying when it comes to the concept of immortal
souls. If the *Chaldean Oracles* are true, then Hekate holds the key to
both a great reunion with the ultimate higher power, and being forever barred from that great union. What do those keys ask of us, if
they are a route to union with this great soul?

The idea of the cosmic soul and the role that Hekate plays as
gatekeeper, potentially allowing or preventing souls from entering, may be uncomfortable for many Witches who left the religious upbringings of their childhood with a similar belief. We must
remember that the *Chaldean Oracles* and the idea of a cosmic soul
reflect a different time and culture, of which we are missing much

context and understanding. It would be a mistake to try to cloister Hekate into the role of the punisher, imagining that Hekate would send us to a proverbial hell for not measuring up. We must remember that we have the freedom to reimagine what the cosmic soul might mean. Maybe it means being the best person we can possibly be, and uniting with the best in other people. It may be that Hekate's keys, immortalized for millennia as a pathway to becoming our best selves, provide the tools for doing just that.

CONNECTING WITH THE KEY KEEPER

If I, as the Witch I am now, could talk to my six-year-old self, I would explain a few things: One, no amount of wishing or imagination will overrule the laws of physics. And that's fine! Two, that little key will not take you back to Tennessee via a literal portal. Yet it did something greater: it opened your curiosity to Magick.

Instead of taking for granted that magick was something that would happen only because I wanted it to, I understood that magick was something I would have to seek. I must have understood that the magickal journey would not be a quick fix.

We Witches serve as key keepers for those who wish to find magick. People come to us for help making sense of confusing or frightening experiences. Seasoned Witches tutor newer Witches. Newer Witches, in turn, find themselves teaching seasoned Witches as well. We continue to open doors for each other, deepening our own understanding and unlocking magick for the world.

But before we can do that, we must unlock ourselves from our own patterns of shame, judgment, and more. We cannot be effective Witches while we are still locked inside proverbial prisons, shaped by culture, personal trauma, or simply not being in touch with our own true wants and desires. This usually won't happen only once.

Throughout the course of a Witch's life, we'll find ourselves unlocking, releasing, and re-releasing ourselves numerous times.

For me, I'd found myself in a space of meh. I'd been a very public Witch for a long time, and while fortunate enough to be so in safety, I cringed when people who didn't identify as Witches asked me about being a Witch. I was tired of explaining myself, being a niche curiosity. I felt that if I couldn't articulate myself perfectly every time, or if I couldn't be constantly available to everyone who had a question about Witchcraft, and if I didn't have every answer, then I was a failure. When I heard the word *Witch*, I no longer felt excited. I felt tired. The key keeper was the aspect of Hekate that I felt the strongest pull toward—but, just as I can't quite place the moment Hekate came into my life, I also can't name the moment when she unlocked me from my meh space. Yet, she appeared as she always had for me: quietly and completely.

I began writing this chapter during a particularly grueling time at my day job. I found myself with little time to even sit at my Hekate altar, let alone write about her. I was staying in a tiny, sparse hotel room in a park-less pocket of a strange city. There was no natural environment to walk through. The area wasn't very safe at night, so I couldn't even walk and gaze at the moon. Again, I'd brought no altar materials or effigies of Hekate. Any magick I would need to create would have to come from me, and my reserves were quite low. But in the last few minutes before I fell asleep on the last night of my trip, I asked Hekate if she would reveal her key-keeper self.

Maybe it was the environment. I was surrounded by people of many different faiths along with several public Witches who were all working for social justice. The theme of the conference was about loving oneself and each other, galvanizing in the face of oppression, and stepping out of the pressures of capitalism. Many of the conversations pointed out that capitalism was forcing us to produce as much as we are able, without any thought to our own humanity. Although I was working the conference and not fully engaging in the discussions, something seeped through. I was collecting discarded coffee cups when, like a key in a lock, the truth clicked.

Yes, my energy and time had been misused—not just by others but also by me. But for the most part, none of this was because others were inherently greedy or unkind, or because I was weak and complicit. In that moment, I realized that we had all been taught by the consumer culture in which we were raised to treat others in the way someone had treated the coffee cups I'd collected—use until they are no longer useful, and then discard them; discard sooner if they don't provide enough. A deep compassion settled into my heart, both for those who I felt had mistreated me and for myself. The roles may have been unbalanced and unfair, but they were merely a reflection of what we'd been taught. Our enemy was not within each other, but in the system grooming us to buy, sell, and consume each other and the planet.

Naming the root of an issue can do a great deal to repair the heart. In naming the root, I released myself from resentment. I can only hope it will help me walk away from such situations in the future and help show other Witches how to preserve themselves as well as the planet.

This was my gift from Hekate the key keeper. I know she has done this and more for others. I'm sure I will need her again, when it's time to break free from something else. If, like Hekate, part of a Witch's role is the ability to unlock magick for individuals or the greater world in general, we first need to ensure we ourselves are free.

Hekate's keys also represent curiosity. A Witch must never presume to know everything. We must continue to lean into our sense of wonder, knowing that behind each locked door is yet another one, needing yet another key to open its secrets. And sometimes, like my experience with the mythical key to Tennessee, the door doesn't exist in the way that we thought it would. In those cases, we can take it as an opportunity to find a different kind of door. I may have stopped looking for a portal to Tennessee, but when I walk into metaphysical stores where my books are sold, I know I became the key to others that I was looking for myself, helping readers open their own doors to magick (or so I hope!).

WORKING WITH THE KEY KEEPER

If you want to work with Hekate the key keeper, start by surrounding yourself with keys, or at least include a few in your magickal work. My favorite keys for this are skeleton keys from vintage or antique stores. Keys that, in my opinion, are especially poignant to Hekate are "junk drawer" keys, with mysterious origins and unknown locks. The keys can be kept on your altar, if you have one. If you don't, keeping them in your pocket, purse, or wallet is another good way. (And there's no reason not to do both, if you're able.)

Before working with any tool, it's good practice to cleanse it and invite the tool to work with you. Not every tool will want to be used magickally, so it's important to get permission first. For keys, cleanse with salt water (don't soak a metal key in water for long, as it will rust), cup the key in your hands, and breathe onto it. This will wake up the key. Hold it tightly in your hands and envision using it as a magickal tool. If you feel a vibration in your hands or if it feels like the key warms up, the key is probably saying yes. Another option is to dangle a pendulum over the key, after designating a certain sway or rotation for the pendulum meaning "yes" and "no." If you feel nothing from the key and the pendulum offers nothing, the specific key may not want to be a magickal object.

If the key is willing to work as a magickal tool, consider doing a small ritual to dedicate it to Hekate. This is best done on either the new or full moon. If you want to use the key in work with chthonic spirits, consider painting the key black or dark blue, as these colors traditionally connect with Hekate's work in the underworld. For other work, such as healing or love or otherwise, let yourself be inspired, selecting colors that particularly resonate with you and the work you want to do. It's also fine to not paint the key. I personally don't, particularly with antique keys.

The following are some suggestions of ways to include Hekate key-keeper energy in your magickal work. Naturally, the best spells come to us organically, so feel free to change these up to suit your specific work. One piece of information that may be helpful: the numbers ten and four are particularly potent in working with Hekate's key-bearer self.[24]

BEGINNING THE WORK

To start, state your intention. It could be something like, "I dedicate this key to Hekate—Kleidoukhos, the key keeper," or something you write yourself. If you're looking for something older and/or more elaborate, this invocation is inspired by Adam Forrest's translation of "The Orphic Hymn to Hekate":

Hekate of the path, I invoke thee,
Beautiful lady of the triple crossroads.
Celestial, chthonia, and marine one,
Lady of the saffron robe,
Lady of the tomb, one who celebrates the mysteries of the dead,
Daughter of destruction, lover of solitude,
She who rejoices in deer,

Nocturnal one, lady of the dogs, invincible queen.
She of the cry of the beast, the wild one,
having an irresistible form.
Bull herder, keeper of the keys of all the universe,
Mistress, guide, bride,
Nurturer of youths, mountain wanderer.
I pray thee, maiden, to be present at this rite of initiation,
Always bestowing graces upon us, the common ones.[25]

A SPELL TO OPEN A SYMBOLIC DOOR

If you've been struggling to get into a certain arena, this spell can help. Perhaps you want to work at a company whose hiring process is notoriously competitive. Maybe you're trying to join a coven and it's going slower than you'd like. Maybe you want to get into a school or some other organization. Maybe you're feeling generally stuck and want to make some changes. Maybe you want to open the door to new love. This spell is best done a few days after the new moon.

If you know what door you want opened (for example, a company or a school), print out an image of it. If what you have in mind doesn't have a sigil, a picture of a door is acceptable. Write on the piece of paper what you want to open with that door.

Make a circle in your magick space with an offering. (I like to offer Hekate garlic for its underground growth, its accessibility, and because I love the smell.) Set the paper effigy and a key in the center of the circle. If the space allows, light four white candles. (Alternatively, if there's a color that better corresponds to the spell, such as green for money matters or red for love, that's also fine. In a pinch, use whatever is available. Battery-operated candles are a fine substitute.)

Recite an invocation to Hekate for assistance, using either the one above or one you create yourself. Be sure to include exactly what you want to happen, such as, "open the door to new love" or "open the door to education" (including the name of the school, if you have it).

Puncture the center of the image with the key and turn it three times to the left.

Burn the paper when you're done and sprinkle the ashes at your front door, bringing that opportunity to you.

Remember, the spell alone is not enough. If you are trying to get that job or into that school, make sure your applications are perfect and that you show up in excellent form for your interviews. If you're trying to open the door to love, keep your online profiles updated and make sure you're getting out and meeting people. Carry the key with you to interviews, dates, and networking opportunities.

A SPELL TO CLOSE A DOOR

Once upon a time, when we closed a door on someone, we removed their number from our address book. Now, we have even more techniques of removing people from our lives, such as blocking their profiles online or taking them out of our phones, but it doesn't erase them from our heart. When we've had a painful time with someone and it appears that they won't be our friend, lover, or colleague anymore, we may find ourselves wondering when they're going to knock on the door and ask for forgiveness. That may never happen, and we do ourselves a favor when we close the door in grace.

A ritual to close the door actually involves a door, as well as a key.

Many of the best spells involve more imagination than the typical ritual tools of flames, altars, and more. As Witches, our imaginations can connect us energetically to other people and places. When you are ready to close the door on a relationship or time in your life, begin by going to your front door. Take a moment to imagine exactly what this person looked like when you last saw them (their clothes, how they wore their hair, if they stood with arms crossed or open, as many details as you can remember). Recall their scent as much as you're able. Recall the last thing they said to you. Try to recall their voice.

Once you have honed your memory of the person, imagine that they are directly outside your front door. It is likely that you will have called a piece of their energetic essence to your home, so this next part is very important.

Open the door, and as loudly as you are able, declare "Goodbye" or "It is done." Close the door swiftly and firmly. Use the key to tap around the doorknob in four places—above, to the right, below, and to the left of the knob. Do this three times.

Place your hand on the door and say, "This door is closed. We take separate paths."

Stand for a moment and imagine that the person vanishes and/ or evaporates from your threshold. You may want to consider doing a ceremonial sweep with a broom, away from your home, when you next leave your house.

If this was a particularly toxic situation, you may want to discard the key when you are done with this working. Be sure to do a ritual to thank the key and release it from its duties. Even holding it and offering a few words of thanks and letting it know the work is done will suffice.

A TALISMAN FOR TRANSITIONS

If you're in a transition in life and are looking to ease the sting of change, charge a key as a transition talisman. Take the key to a crossroads and hold it tightly between your palms for ten seconds. Open your palms and speak the following over the key:

> Triple-headed Hekate,
> who is aware of my enterprise,
> you come as a helper,
> and with the chants and arts
> of the magicians and Mother Earth,
> you instruct the Witches in the potent herbs.
> Aid me now as I walk these crossroads.
> Open the door to comfort and ease.
> Bless this key with your guiding spirit.[26]

Carry the key with you in a pocket or on your key ring. When the transition begins to feel hard, hold the key tight and remember that you have a guide in Hekate to show you through this tricky time.

OPENING THE DOOR TO A NEW PATH

When you're ready to open to a new path, take your anointed key to a physical crossroads. Turn your back to the crossroads for a moment and think of the path you are leaving behind. List everything about it for which you are grateful, every lesson and more. Turn and face the crossroads, holding the key to your brow, your heart, and each foot, declaring the following in turn:

Brow: I open my mind to the new way,
Heart: I open my heart to receive gifts of the journey,
Left and right feet: I open myself to a new path,
Guided by the great Hekate, the blessed Kleidoukhos,
To open the door, to show me the way.

Make an offering to Hekate, such as some of her traditional food offerings, or a poem or song in her honor. Pass over the crossroads without looking back. An easy way to do this is to make your crossroads an intersection near your home. Cross the street and walk around the block to head home.

If you cannot or do not want to leave your home, this working can be done at a doorway.

RITUAL FOR GREATER UNDERSTANDING OF HEKATE OR OTHER MYSTERIES

Leave four or ten keys as part of your permanent altar to her. Breathe on the keys regularly, reminding them of their work. Be sure to journal dreams or moments of powerful synchronicity, as they may be holding clues to the deeper mysteries Hekate wants to share with you.

KEYS AS MAGICKAL PROTECTION

Don't underestimate the power of dedicating your household and/or car keys to Hekate! To do this, regularly anoint them with soil from a crossroads. You can also gently wave them through a candle you use on her altar, one designated as Hekate's torch. Recite the following:

Star-coursing, heavenly torchbearer,
Fire-breathing goddess,

Four-faced, four-named,
Four roads' mistress.
Hail, goddess! Protect my house, home, transport,
and all those within it.[27]

If you are asking for specific help from the crossroads or the torchbearer, be sure to make regular offerings, either on the altar or at the crossroads.

CHAPTER EIGHT

Mother, Foster Mother, and Fertility Goddess

There are so many names and aspects that she holds. She will come to me as a fierce, loving grandmother or wise woman. I love, respect, and cherish that about her. Sometimes, when I'm reading Tarot or oracle cards for clients or while I'm in ceremony, she will nudge me to channel messages for folx who need it. She comes especially to those in need, who are experiencing grief, heartache, anxiety, or indecision, or who are at a crossroads on their life path. I've felt her presence when doing work related to death, supporting folx or creatures transitioning to the other side. Hecate is all about the night realms, the moon, stars, shadows, and everything in between.

—THORNE DAVIS, MODERN DEVOTEE OF HEKATE

It's often thought that Witches have loved and revered ubiquitous mother-goddess figures for as long as there have been Witches. Today, many Witches refer to the goddess much in the way that many followers of Abrahamic faiths refer to God: this goddess is a feminine figure who is ever powerful, all-forgiving, and never fully knowable. There's nothing inherently wrong with this, but such a viewpoint is quite new in contrast to much of human history. Pre-Christian religions all over the world had great mother figures in their pantheons, but how powerful they were varied widely. The ancient Greeks saw Gaia as a powerful mother goddess figure, but it was the hypermasculine Zeus who ruled the other gods. Mother goddesses weren't always in charge. Nor were they always kind, giving, or protective. In many cases, mother goddesses could be elusive, cruel, or indifferent to the plights of humans. Many, like Hekate, could be both.

One of Hekate's roles was as a guardian of children. In one image at the ancient Greek town of Lagina, it is Hekate who gives the stone replacement to the Titan Kronos to devour, protecting the infant Zeus.[1] Hekate is also said to have shared a special bond with women who struggle to conceive, or whose children die prematurely.[2] Hekate's myths don't often have her raising children, but that may be a function of a time when people rarely lived to old age and frequently died in childbirth. It's possible that the idea of mothering was not connected only with those who gave birth and may have been a community role. Siblings, cousins, aunts, uncles, and grandparents likely joined in to help with the child-rearing when a parent died early. Given that Hekate was also often referred to as one who watched from afar, she may have represented the idea of a departed mother who would always watch over her children.

Hekate takes an important mother role in what is arguably the most famous of the ancient Greek myths.

HEKATE AND PERSEPHONE

In the myth of Persephone's abduction, Hekate has a crucial role in helping the grieving Demeter find her missing daughter as well as being an aid to Persephone while she resides in the dark, cold realm of Hades. As a child, I recall seeing an animated film portraying Persephone's abduction. Although I was young, I easily understood its themes: a scared girl, a grieving mother, the changing of the seasons. Its relatability and easy adaptation are perhaps why it has endured throughout the centuries. Yet its telling is often titled "The Rape of Persephone," an understandably unnerving title. In another version of the story, Persephone was abducted when she grasped a narcissus, a flower whose myth warns against focusing too much on the self. This flower pulled her through to the underworld, perhaps suggesting that Persephone aided in her own undoing. A more contemporary version of the story involves Persephone being led by her own curiosity to the realm of Hades and staying there of her own volition to better learn the mysteries of life and death, much to her mother's chagrin. In one of my favorite memes, a cartoon of a loving couple, Persephone and Hades, cuddle in bed together, dreading their upcoming separation. But if we think of this tale as a story of the changing of the seasons, it may be a reflection of an ancient people viewing the upcoming winter as an assault on their land, to which their own life and death were inextricably tied.

What is often forgotten in retellings of this myth is Hekate's role in it. Not only does she appear with the literal torches that hallmark her nickname of Torchbearer, but she alone comes to aid Demeter. She doesn't only relay the information she has about Persephone; she accompanies Demeter to Helios to uncover the truth. In ancient artists' renditions of the encounter, Hekate and her torches lead Persephone to Hermes, who will take the girl to Demeter after her period in Hades. It's also thought that Hekate filled the role of a surrogate mother to Persephone during her time in the underworld, being a literal light to the girl during a dark time in her life. When Persephone emerges from the underworld, Hekate walks with her to meet Hermes, the god who ultimately takes her back to the surface to reunite with her mother.

Persephone was also worshipped by the Romans, in two primary ways: as the maiden or Kore (which means young girl), and as queen of the underworld. Kore is slender, beautiful, young, and associated with symbols of fertility: pomegranates, grain, corn, and narcissus—the flower that lured her. As queen of the underworld, she is the mature goddess who reigns over dead souls, a guide for the rare living being who visits the underworld, a queen who claims for herself what she wants.[3] Rites honoring Persephone, or the Roman Kore, included processions in the fall that involved pausing at numerous shrines that reflected the powers of generation both of Demeter and Kore and those of the death god, Hades (called Pluto by the Romans).[4] This suggests that Demeter's mysteries were deeper than the soil, connecting her with human mortality and the afterlife.[5]

While Hekate was certainly a companion of Persephone and was most often described as such, Hekate and Persephone may have at times been considered two faces of the same goddess, Hekate the face of a period of darkness and Persephone the face of the goddess returning to earth. Hekate is a face of the triune with Demeter and Persephone as well as the wise auntie taking care of the young, confused child—being her and caring for her at the same time.

As a mother goddess tied tightly to both Demeter and Persephone, Hekate may represent the voice of the parent within the child's head: the memory of the parent's lessons, support, or criticisms when they are separated from them, whether for an afternoon with a playmate or once they have moved on with their own lives.

In another sense, the Persephone myth may represent the relationship between spouse, parent, and child, perhaps for one person finding balance between embodying those roles in their own life. Persephone's suffering may be familiar to many: being pulled in multiple directions by many obligations, feeling dismay at not being "enough" for all of them. In that perspective, Hekate stands in the middle, asking nothing of the person in turmoil, but simply being there as a comfort and guide.

In some interpretations, Persephone represents someone emerging from illness with a greater awareness of the meaning of life, possibly even an awareness of another way of being, which can be symbolized as having Hekate as a companion.[6] In this view, Hekate may represent a coping mechanism for those who suffered trauma in childhood. She might also represent the role of the therapist, teacher, or counselor helping a child through those situations. Hekate may manifest again in similar roles when we walk through our dark times as an adult.

Meanwhile, Demeter, as earth goddess, holds the powers of life and death, and growth. Demeter was credited for blessing the world, but more famous for cursing it while deep in her grief. She is perhaps more commonly identified as a parent than as an embodiment of the earth and seasons. It is her grief and insurmountable desire to be reunited with her beloved daughter that make her relatable to many. Yet Demeter's curse is less an aggressive action against the earth than a withdrawal. She simply refuses to do her work until things are made right. Demeter is not known for what she does but rather what she does not do. Sometimes the act of stepping back is more powerful than stepping forward.

Finally, Hekate holds a small but crucial role in this myth. Without Hekate, Demeter could not have seen through her grief to approach Helios. Hekate is the grounded presence that sees through the troubling time, offering solutions and pushing those in power to help those who are suffering.

To me, the Persephone myth speaks of humans trying to understand a changing environment. Could this myth be far older than ancient Greece, perhaps explaining the end of the ice age, when the warming climate brought forth new seasons? Could it also represent the development of agriculture? In either case, Hekate represents a way forward, inserting hope into a difficult time. Perhaps now, as the earth faces devastating climate changes, inspiration through and devotion to Hekate could help us find ways to live in harmony with the planet.

The possibilities for the meaning of Hekate's role in the Persephone myth are endless. Yet, the ancient gods were rarely all-powerful. Even Zeus had limits. Hekate could not command Hades to release Persephone, nor could she designate how long the young goddess would have to spend away from her mother. Still, she offered what support she could. But although she was not all-powerful, Hekate was not powerless. She found purpose in the darkness and cared for those who were suffering and could not help themselves. Perhaps this is one reason why Witches are often drawn to mother-goddess figures. We so very often want to care for others. Even Witches attracted to the most baneful magick are often performing it on behalf of someone else who was hurt or mis-treated. Like Hekate, we are not all-powerful, but we can often find a way to soften a hard situation, through either our magick or our determined presence.

HEKATE: MOTHER AND FERTILITY GODDESS

Even if the gods had limits, the powers they did have were immense, controlling major elements on the earth. While Hekate is associated more with the night than the day and thought to be a goddess of the moon and the underworld, there was no shortage of examples in which she was invoked as a powerful, all-purpose deity whose patronage extended to every corner of existence.

In Ovid's *Metamorphoses*, the main character, Lucius, who is defined by his interest in the magickal arts, purifies himself by dipping his head into the sea seven times. He offers a prayer to a supreme goddess, one who may be Hekate.[7] She appears before him, emerging from the sea, wearing a wreath on her head with flowers of every kind, a round disc on her brow, and a many-colored robe. In her right hand she carries a bronze rattle, in her left a gold dish with a serpent curled around it. She responds:

"Behold, Lucius, I am here, moved by your prayers,
the mother of nature, the mistress of all the elements,
the first child of the ages, the greatest of the powers,
the queen of the dead, ruler of the heavens,
the singular form of all the gods and goddesses.
Who, with my nod, arranges the gleaming summit of the
     heavens,
the wholesome blasts of sea-wind and the bitter silences of
     the Underworld.
Whose command the whole earth venerates, unparalleled,
in many forms, a variety of rituals, and in multiple names . . .[8]

The goddess goes on listing the many different names she has in different parts of the world. If this is Hekate, this passage speaks to her antiquity and expanse. It may also speak to a universal idea, perhaps at the time, that all life comes from a feminine source. This force can be great and bountiful, but it can also be terrifying. It is the same power that births, heals, and kills. In short, it is the energy that says, "I brought you into this world, and I can take you out of it." It is the ultimate mother figure, a title that carries a complex web of identities.

In many ancient traditions, a mother goddess was synonymous with the earth's natural cycles. She would be credited for the crop cycle's productivity or blamed for its failure. Appeasing such a goddess was believed essential to ensuring a bountiful harvest. Hekate's rites included honoring her as both a mother and a fertility goddess, but perhaps not in a way we would recognize. Those who worshipped the fertile mother also honored her as a death bringer, acknowledging that without death there could be no life, and the seeming or actual death at the end of each crop cycle was essential for new life to come in the following year.

Hekate's association with the title "one hundred" may refer to a hundred lunar months of corn growth, connecting her to the crop's life cycle. By the end of the seventh century, the fame of this triple corn goddess in her many forms spread abroad, also becoming associated with grim and bestial deities.[9] The change from a primarily bountiful deity to one much more somber or even frightening may have been sparked by famine, war, or disease. A goddess like Hekate, whose history reveals her as both benevolent and horrifying, carries the experiences of long-ago people experiencing gentle and terrible events.

Whether great or frightening, Hekate was frequently revered as a fertility goddess. At certain Greek sites, Hekate's torches were carried around freshly sown fields to promote their fertility.[10] It's also thought that these rites were believed to be more successful if the conductors of the rites were themselves fertile, and therefore were led by people of child-bearing age.[11] These rites may suggest that Hekate was a goddess strongly associated with fertility, as well as death and decomposition. The old corn stocks wither, disintegrate, and die, and in doing so become the compost that nurtures the soil, encouraging future growth. If Demeter is the ripe corn and Persephone is new growth, death and decay, and regeneration, Hekate is the journey from both life to death and death to life—the torchbearer who lights and guides the way through the liminal realms.

If new crops grow from the decomposing forms of the old, a goddess of fertility would periodically walk through the underworld. Therefore, Hekate easily held the roles of both goddess of new life as well as one who walked with ghosts. It may be this fertility goddess role that led to her patronage of all other things. It was also one of Hekate's oldest and most central roles.

Hekate was known as *kourotrophos* (meaning "nurse" or "child nurturer") to all living things.[12] Some of the original images of Hekate mirror the famous seated "great mother" of Çatal Hüyük, an ancient city in what is now Turkey. She may have inherited other ancient traits from the fertility goddesses who figure prominently in every period of Asia Minor's archeology.[13] In Hesiod's poetry, her functions were as universal as those of the Greek goddess Athena, some of which included law and victory, but also child-rearing.[14] A figure adjacent to Hekate found on a lekythos relief holds a flower that could connect her to fertility.[15] Some painters depicted her as a guardian of marriage.[16]

Hekate's association with fertility may also come through other goddesses. The Greek historian and philosopher Strabo believed Hekate belonged in a circle of cults in Phrygia, a kingdom in Asia Minor existing from 1200–700 BCE, of which the chief figure was an earth goddess and orgiastic rituals a marked characteristic.[17] Artemis was depicted as a great mother in images from these same cults. However, it may be fair to point out that Hekate is often called Artemis, but Artemis is not often called Hekate. At some point, Artemis evolved into the well-known virgin huntress of the moon, a fit sister for the solar god Apollo, and it was Hekate who relieved Artemis of her outgrown traits, including that of fertility.[18] Asteria, the star goddess and a mother to Hekate, gave shelter to the goddess Leto when she birthed Zeus's twins, who was given no rest because Hera had cursed her for having relations with Zeus. Asteria was therefore believed to look over those giving birth, as well as those in dangerous or transitory circumstances. A goddess from the ancient Greek province of Arcadia who was associated with fertility was specifically called Despoina-Hekate. Despoina-Hekate's name was also given to doorways and gateways, a liminal place often associated with fertility and birth.[19] Hekate was on hand at birth, when the soul joins the body, and at death, when it leaves it. Birth and death were hand in hand, soul in soul.

Hekate, along with other deities of the night, was often associated with the life cycle and fertility of human beings, as well as dark magick and the underworld.[20] People of child-bearing age were likely the conductors of fertility rites, perhaps under the belief that the rites would be more successful if the active participants were the ones who stood to gain the rewards of the ritual.[21] This may lead some modern practitioners to believe that Hekate is a specific patroness of women. While there is certainly nothing wrong with women, cis or trans, finding special connection with Hekate because of her roles that are frequently associated with women, it's important to note that Hekate is not *only* a goddess for women. Different religious rites and cultural practices in ancient Greece suggest they acknowledged a wider spectrum of gender identity than simply man and woman. While unpacking these rites and practices is beyond the scope of this book, this is important to remember when embracing modern Witchcraft in general and Hekate practices in particular. It is quite likely that Hekate was traditionally associated with a variety of gender identities and continues to be a patroness available to Witches of all genders.

If the work was successful and the fertility goddess was pleased, the gifts she could give were boundless. The writer Hesiod says of Hekate:

And she is good to stand by horsemen, whom she will: and to those whose business is in the grey discomfortable sea, and who pray to Hecate and the loud-crashing Earth-Shaker, easily the glorious goddess gives great catch, and easily she takes it away as soon as seem, if so she will. She is good in the byre with Hermes to increase the stock. The droves of kine and wide herds of goats and flocks of fleecy sheep, if she will, she increases from a few, or makes many to be less. So, then, albeit her mother's only child, she is honored amongst all the deathless gods. And the son of Cronos made her a nurse of the young who after that day saw with their eyes the light of all-seeing Dawn. So from the beginning she is a nurse of the young, and these are her honors.[22]

JOURNEYING WITH THE MOTHER GODDESS

There is a common sentiment in contemporary Witchcraft that goddesses must either be mother goddesses, who are all about sweetness and light and kindness, or "dark" goddesses, who are only about scary things. It is assumed that they cannot be both. Therefore, when inviting a mother goddess into their lives and expecting the sugar sweetness of the former, new Witches are often confused by spates of bad luck or other tough lessons. Inviting such a goddess could only bring joy, right? But when I teach classes on these goddesses, I ask parents in the room to raise their hands and then ask, "Would your kids say you are always sweet and light?" They always laugh and say no (usually "hell no"). I don't think anyone expects a mother, or any parent, to be nice all the time. If they were, they wouldn't be doing their job. Why shouldn't we expect this same complexity in a mother goddess?

The ancients seemed to understand the textured roles of mother goddesses. They likely accepted the messiness and contradictions, understanding that mother goddesses could be difficult and fertility goddesses weren't magickal wish-granters. The fertility goddesses did not represent abundance so much as process, relationship, sacrifice, and faith. Those who work closely with the earth, even if that's a simple garden, have experienced the ebbs and flows of the relationship with the fertility goddess. Likewise, if you ask anyone who has been through the trials of fertility treatments, you'll know that fertility isn't granted because you want it, even if you take all the steps the book or doctor prescribes. Like the goddess descending to the underworld, the fertility goddess sometimes vanishes from a situation without any clear explanation. Will she bring the crops back next year? Will she help with a baby? Where did she go? We don't know.

Modern Witchcraft has had an almost hyper-fixation with pregnancy and birth, the ubiquitous goddess regularly shown as peaceful and pregnant. The neo-Pagan wheel of the year mythology has an incessant focus on the fertility of the earth and feminine procreation. It comes from a beautiful place, the desire to honor the feminine divine and the bodies of feminine persons that have been demonized. Still, this intense focus can be isolating and even demoralizing. Many Witches do not identify as female. Many are in same-sex relationships. Some Witches are not sexual at all. Not every Witch is born with a uterus. Not every Witch with a uterus can even use it for procreation. Plenty of Witches don't want to give birth or raise children at all. Where is the space for these Witches?

Hekate has an answer for that, too.

Like Hekate at Persephone's side in the underworld, the classic Witch has traditionally been a foster or surrogate parent, a role that frequently plays out in our own communities. In countless fairy tales and other stories, the childless aunt or eccentric neighbor who also tends to have magickal powers is a beacon of safety or inspiration or a strong, formal role in the child's life. Modern Witchcraft frequently embraces unofficial adoption, embracing the idea of chosen family in Witchcraft communities. While this can provide plenty of other complications, many Witchcraft groups label one or more of their leaders as a mother- and/or father-type character. Witches often mentor younger or inexperienced Witches. And almost every Witch I know is involved in some kind of animal rescue, caring for animals as their own children.

But more so than biology, taking care of children or not, the mother goddess brings hard truths. Just as the parent can deliver a message to their child that no one else dares to utter, this guise of Hekate makes us aware of parts of ourselves we need to face, shadow issues we must combat, areas that need healing, parts that need motivation.

Honoring Hekate the Mother

To involve Hekate the mother in the work you want to do, the following rite may help.

For three months, on both the new moon and the full moon, create time to look at the moon. This may be challenging on cloudy nights, so trying on either side of the actual day is alright, too. This can be particularly hard on new moon nights; just do the best you can. Ideally, this would happen outside. If the weather is bad or you live in a place where you can't be outside privately or safely, doing this at a window where you can see the moon (or roughly where it is on cloudy nights) is also fine.

Say the following aloud, as though you were speaking directly to the moon:

> For to this day, whenever any one of us on earth
> Offers rich sacrifices and prays for favor according to custom,
> We call upon Hekate.
> Great honor comes full easily to those
> Whose prayers the goddess receives favorably,
> And she bestows wealth upon them,
> For the power surely is with her.[23]

Perform this spell on both the new moon and full moon for three months. Given the connections with the harvest time, consider performing this during the months surrounding the harvest. Depending on your region, this may vary. Where I live, the harvest months are August, September, and October. However, if you want to make this connection at a different time, there is no wrong time to do it.

After this three-month rite, consider doing this rite whenever you feel you need to check back in with Hekate.

Spell to Protect Someone You Care About

This next spell is inspired by one I learned from Hoodoo practitioners.

Take a picture of the person, people, or animal you want Hekate to protect. This can certainly be yourself. Wrap the image in a small piece of cotton or silk fabric and place in a small jar. Adhere a black candle to the top of the jar. (An easy way to do this is to melt some of the wax on the bottom of the candle and firmly affix it to the jar lid. Avoid using glues, as many are combustible.) Light the candle and say the following protection prayer:

> As the dark of the new moon cloaks the great Selene,
> May the blessed darkness prevent evil, harm, or misfortune
> From finding [name].
> May they be held in Hekate's sacred hands,
> In safety, peace, and blessings.

Make an offering to Hekate, whether through libation, poetry, or song. Saying the hymn from the previous ritual is a fine offering. Light the candle for a few minutes a day while saying the protection prayer. When the candle has all melted (wax should cover at least part of the jar), consider doing the rite again with a new candle. The idea is for the black wax to coat the jar so that evil or harm cannot find the thing you care about. This can also be done for a business, endeavor, or social group.

Spell for Fertility

Capture some moon water (see page 52). If you are growing plants or crops near your home, sprinkle the water on the plants at night as you say the following prayer:

As the moon grows from sliver to full
So may you grow strong and full
With Hekate's blessings, breath, and kiss.

If you are trying to become pregnant yourself or with a partner, use this water in your bath or shower, paying special attention to washing your womb or testicle area.

Spell for Enterprise and Growth

The moon-water working in the last spell can be used for enterprise and growth as well. However, you can also take it a step further by physically encouraging growth.

Take a bulb of garlic and whisper to it everything that you want your enterprise to be. Say, for example, you are running a business. Describe the business to the garlic bulb as if the bulb itself were the business: "You are a web design company. You serve artistic clients." Tell the bulb how many people it serves, and what you want to see happen in the future. For example, "You have fifteen clients. In a year's time, you will have doubled the number of clients you currently have."

Break the bulb apart, plant the cloves in a pot with potting soil, and leave in a sunny area. Water regularly so that the soil stays damp, but not soggy. When you water the garlic, whisper over it,

Hekate, bless this endeavor.
Hekate, nurture this endeavor to grow.

When the garlic produces shoots, snip them and make them part of your offering to Hekate.

CHAPTER NINE

Hekate's Grimoire

And may the altars, where at the elders gather, blaze in honor of venerable men. Thus may their state be regulated well, if they hold in awe mighty Zeus, and most of all, Zeus the warden of guest-right, who by venerable enactment guideth destiny aright. And that other guardian always be renewed we pray: and that Artemis-Hekate watch over the childbed of their women.

—AESCHYLUS, *THE SUPPLIANT MAIDENS*[1]

ekate's history as a goddess of Witches is indeed complex, and again, we must remember that she has roots in many diverse cultures and is not solely Greek in origin. It is sometimes thought that some of the features in ancient Greek Witchcraft were inherited from Egypt, features that included practicing magick not just as protection from evil, but harnessing both good and evil to achieve one's goals, and the belief in magickal power being linked to certain words, gestures, and rituals.[2] While we may not have access to many, if any, of these rituals today, it does show us that Hekate has a legacy of responding to rites made in her honor. We may also surmise that the use of words, prayers, and hymns is quite powerful when invoking Hekate.

Such hymns were traditionally offered not only to Hekate but also other deities such as Apollo, Hermes, Helios, Aphrodite, and Typhon. She was often summoned as a trifecta with either Selene and Artemis or Demeter and Persephone. These partnering gods were not always kind; Typhon in particular was described as a grisly monster banished by Zeus to the underworld. The Greeks seemed to believe there was power and purpose in summoning gods that were scarier than others.

In ancient times, Hekate was often sought out for revelation, divination and oracular messages, summoning a spirit to use in other magick, enticing help from gods, and preventing a god's interference. Other Hekate spells were designed for sexual attraction, favor and victory, memory and foreknowledge, healing, and being released from spells. She was also invoked for silencing a competitor or inflicting harm on an enemy. Hekate rites often involved horoscopes and astrology. Witches would frequently have Hekate bless amulets or other trinkets, which could be used in other spells.[3] Hekate's name was often inscribed on magickal amulets or other charms, which were filled with herbs sacred to Hekate.[4]

Then as now, spellcasting is the work of using spirit and ritual to make a desired change in your life. Is it time to bring in love? Maybe money is tight and you could use increased prosperity. Perhaps there are negative energies in your life that you would like to eliminate. Change in a person's life via the casting of a spell is the essence of Witchcraft. As a goddess of Witches, Hekate has a long history with assisting in spells.

This chapter contains spells and rituals that may be helpful when working with Hekate. Now, no one *has* to cast spells in order to know Hekate, but because many people who work with Hekate like to cast spells, I have included many in this section. Take inspiration from these and make them your own. Don't hesitate to add or improvise.

Remember always that magick is a creative act, and it is my belief that Witches are artists, even if they don't practice any other kind of art but Witchcraft. Leave your personal imprint on the work that you do. As a practical and environmental tactic, using what you have, harvesting things sustainably, or reusing older items is always a good thing to do.

TO BEGIN: MAKE AN OFFERING TO HEKATE

If we'd like Hekate's, or any god's help, we need to make it worth their while. To do this, begin with an offering.

As with any offering to any deity, keeping it personal is key. I always find it easier to imagine that this goddess was a person. If I didn't know my friend Kanani beyond her reputation but I still wanted to win her favor, offering her ice cream or coffee would be a good start, as she is very public about her love for both. However, because I've known Kanani for many years, I also happen to know that she tried baked brie at my house a few years ago and loved it. Now, other people might make her day by bringing her baked brie ... but she expects it from me, as it's part of our history. Hekate is well known for her love of garlic and honey, but perhaps at your house she craves the raspberry jam you canned last year. If you feel called to spoon a bit of that onto your offering plate, don't avoid the impulse because it's not "traditional."

Food and drink are, and have historically been, what people have offered gods in many different cultures, perhaps with the belief that the gods are going to eat the essence, or the fragrance, of the offered goods. Preparing a meal or a plate of food for a god or goddess is very satisfying and certainly brings great results, but it's not the only way to do things.

Use your natural talents—or rather, do things that you enjoy. I'm not famous for my singing voice, but I love to sing. While I never made it as a Broadway performer, when I sing for the gods, people tell me I sound wonderful. I think it's because I'm singing out of love for the work and for them, not for any performative reasons. Writing poems, drawing pictures, planting or arranging flowers, even writing code for a glorious website dedicated to them are all invaluable gifts of the gods. Let inspiration strike—and if it doesn't, feel free to arrange a plate of offerings from the list that follows. Here are a few things Hekate is known to be particularly fond of:

- Garlic
- Wine
- Onions
- Cakes (anything sweet)
- Images of dogs (particularly black ones), oxen, snakes, or ewes
- Keys
- Candles
- Oak wood, leaves, or acorns
- Honey
- Herbs (see below)

HERBS HISTORICALLY SACRED TO HEKATE

Hekate has a strong connection with herbs, both for their powers to heal as well as to poison. Like Hekate, many herbs can embody the powers of both life and death. Hekate was especially associated with herbs growing in cemeteries.[5] The following herbs are sacred to Hekate and may be used to decorate the rites or spell vehicles dedicated to her. *As an additional note, these herbs are not suggested here for ingestion or making ointments for the skin.* They are listed with the recommendation that they be used as offerings to Hekate. Particularly as some of these are poisonous, it is fine to use an image of the plant in your ritual space rather than expose yourself, family members or housemates, or pets by bringing these plants into your home. The nonpoisonous plants can be worn in amulets, but some can cause skin irritation. If you have an allergy to any of these, select another herb! No matter what, take care to research each herb before using it. It's always best to use herbs that grow near you or that are sustainably harvested. The gods would prefer that we preserve our planet rather than pillage it in their name.

- Aconite (*Aconitum napellus* [poisonous if ingested or handled without gloves])
- Asphodel (*Asphodelus albus*)
- Basil (*Ocimum basilicum*)
- Cassidony (*Lavandula stoechas*)
- Chamomile (*Matricaria chamomilla*)
- Dittany (*Dictamnus albus*)
- Ginger (*Zingiber officinale*)
- Greenbrier (*Smilax rotundifolia*)
- Hedge mustard (*Sisymbrium officinale*)
- Laurel or bay leaves (*Laurus nobilis*)
- Lion's foot (*Nabalus serpentarius*)
- Mandrake (*Mandragora officinarum* [poisonous if ingested])
- Oak (*Quercus robur* [poisonous if ingested])
- Poppy (*Papaver setigerum*)
- Saffron (*Crocus sativus*)
- Common Sage (*Salvia officinalis*)
- Verbena (*Verbena officinalis*)

Offerings to Hekate can be left on an altar you have created for her, at a crossroads, or any other place you feel called to.

INVOCATIONS TO HEKATE

Because Hekate has historically been summoned through prayer, hymns, and otherwise, using some of her old invocations will bring a great deal of power to your rites with her. Naturally, you can certainly write your own, as personal inspiration is a powerful tool. If you decide to write your own invocations, consider preserving them (perhaps in a magickal journal, on a computer, or in the cloud) and use them repeatedly. A great deal of strength grows in incantations when they are used numerous times.

A few historical incantations can be found below:

> Around you turns the nature of the world . . .
> you have created all cosmic things.[6]

You are the beginning and the end: you alone rule over everything, for all things are from you and all things end, eternal one, in you.[7]

> All hail the many-named mother,
> Hail mighty Hekate, the gatekeeper.
> Shape my life with your glowing torch,
> Enrich it with many blessings,
> And purge sickness and evil from it,
> When my soul is enraged over small things,
> Bless me with your healing rituals.
> I pray to be guided by your gentle hand,
> When I am weary, be my shield and guide,
> Hail the many-named mother,
> Hail mighty Hekate, the gatekeeper.

I invoke you, Hekate of the crossroads, the three-faced lady,
Saffron-cloaked goddess of the cosmos, the underworld,
and the ocean,
Walker among the tombs, reveling in the mysteries of the dead,
Daughter of destruction, lover of the wild,
Night mother, protector of canines, the greatest queen,
Wild woman, primal, irresistible,
Key keeper of all the world,
Great lady, I humbly ask for your presence at my sacred rites.

Oh three-faced Selene, be with me now.
Graciously hear my prayer,
Cloak of night, the maiden moon,
Who rides upon the fiercest beasts,
You who dance in triple forms,
And revel among the stars,
You are Justice, you are the Fates,
You are fate, you are challenge,
You are the dangerous one, you are Justice,
You hold the monsters in chains,
Oh serpent-haired and girdled one,
She who sups on the blood of the living,
And feasts on the hearts of those who died too young,
Grave walker and she who can drive to madness,
Join me now, help me in my rites.[8]

DEVELOPING BASIC MAGICKAL ABILITY

Like strengthening a muscle takes time and effort, Witchcraft does as
well. Spells can work the first time you try to cast one, but you'll find
more consistent success if you treat Witchcraft as a craft, practicing it
regularly and focusing on making it better each time. There are many

ways to become a Witch, but one is through building a relationship with a deity. Hekate, as we have learned, is a great one given that she is a powerful Witch herself. To develop this relationship and increase your magickal ability, perform some of the routine spells below.

CHARGE UP UNDER THE FULL MOON

Ideally, you'd do this spell outside and barefoot on full moon nights. If you can't be outside, practicing by your window is acceptable.

Focusing on the moon, breathe in and imagine that you are connected to it, and each pore of your body is filling up with moonlight. Chant Hekate's name, in a long, solo tone: *Heh——kah——tay——*. Breathe in deeply and intonate Hekate's name again. Do this for ten minutes or so. It may be helpful to set a timer initially. Ten minutes can seem much longer when doing meditation or magick than it does in the rest of your daily activities.

After intoning Hekate's name, stand in silence with your eyes closed, but knowing you are still in sight of the moon and still being filled by its light. Do this every full moon for the first three months while working with Hekate. In the future, you may not need to do it every month, but may find it helpful to easily reconnect when you feel you have had periods of time when Hekate felt far from you.

Especially in the early days of doing this work, be sure to keep a journal of thoughts and unusual experiences that happen during the day. Make sure also to make note of dreams you have during this time.

CLEANSING SELF OF NEGATIVITY

On waning or new moons, select a black candle for your ritual (black because it absorbs). Before lighting the candle, run it over your body like a lint roller while saying the following chant:

In the name of the dark goddess,
the blessed mother,
The sacred serpent,
I shed this foul luck
Like the creature sheds its skin.

If there's something in particular you want out of your life (a bad habit, a problem with a coworker, even a toxic relationship), etch onto the candle a word or two describing it, or the initials of the person you want to stay away from you.

Burn this candle every night until it's burned all the way down. Remember to extinguish the candle when leaving the room or going to sleep. Relight the candle the next day, and every day following, until the candle has finished burning. When the remaining wax has cooled, take the remains to a garbage can at a crossroads (urban areas tend to have garbage cans on corners that are great for this kind of work) and break the wax in half, away from you. Throw the remains in the garbage can and return home without looking back.

Make an offering to Hekate afterward.

MOON WATER

Making and using moon water is beneficial to both spells and your relationship with Hekate. Water is one of the key ingredients in magick. Used for ritual baths, anointing for protection, and to mark a sacred space before doing magickal work, moon water is also likely the most inexpensive, accessible ingredient you can use in a spell. Some people prefer to use holy water, which can be obtained from a Catholic church, for free, although it's kind to make a small donation to the church as a sign of gratitude. Florida water, which can be gotten in many drug stores and metaphysical stores, or ordered online, is another favorite option. Some magick workers only ever use distilled water or well water. I find that tap water is perfectly fine.

If you would like to charge water with the energies of Hekate, there are several ways to do this depending on what you want to use the water for. The different phases of the moon carry different qualities. You may decide to make magick water that corresponds with all of them. Water can turn funky if left alone for too long, so if you're not sure you want to use the water right away, consider freezing it. Consider making use of your freezer's ice tray and making individual cubes of Hekate moon water, which can be thawed and used individually when you're ready to use them. (Never be afraid to include modern technology when working on your spells!)

ANOTHER METHOD OF MAKING MOON WATER

As discussed earlier in the book, capturing the reflection of the moon in a bowl of water will instantly empower the water with the moon. This can be challenging in areas with a lot of cloud cover. I live in the Pacific Northwest, where it is almost always cloudy for several months of the year. I have to do the best I can on these nights! If you can't do this because of a scheduling conflict or cloud cover, set a dish of water in your backyard or on your windowsill for three days: the night before the moon you want to use, the night of the moon, and the night after the moon phase has turned. For waxing or waning moons, you can perform this at any time during the waxing or waning time. Consider adding a pinch of salt or a piece of quartz crystal. Some prefer to add their favorite essential oils to the water. I don't do that at this phase, as the different oils have different magickal connotations and my goal is to make a basic water that will suffice for any magickal work I want to do with Hekate.

When setting the water out, ask Hekate to bless it. A suggested incantation might be:

Hekate, mistress of the night,
Kiss this water for magickal might.

Choose the moon you want to use for moon water. All of them will bring the powers of Hekate, but certain moons are better for some work than others:

- Full moon: completion work, fertility, attraction, clarity, revealing truths, guidance
- Waxing moon: growth, abundance, focus, drive, healing through garnering strength
- Waning moon: banishing, removal, separation, releasing, healing through surrender
- Dark moon (new moon): secrecy, protection, curse work, bindings

Make an offering to Hekate each night you charge the moon water.

A FULL MOON SPELL: FOR GENERAL MAGICKAL POWER, GUIDED BY HEKATE

For the two nights prior to and the night of the full moon, do a ritual bath that includes full-moon water. If you're able to be outside in the nighttime fully nude, that is ideal. If you're not able to be outside, doing this work in the shower is fine. If your hair is long enough, make sure your hair is unbound (no ponytails, buns, or the like).

Cover yourself with the water. Let out three howls. Then stand in silence for a time while you let the water air dry on your skin. Envision the powers of the moon and Hekate seeping into your pores.

When you have completed your work, dress in clean, simple clothing and make a luscious offering to Hekate—maybe wine, warm milk, or lamb's meat.

A WANING MOON SPELL:
A HEKATE PURIFICATION RITE

If you've been surrounded by negativity or feel like bad luck has been following you, or if you've been down in the dumps for a bit and want to break the flow of negativity, this spell can cleanse and release this stuff so that you can move forward with more positive intention and flow.

Dip three candles in wine or grape juice and light them. Using waning-moon water and a rosemary sprig, wet the sprig of rosemary and brush it over your head and along your limbs and torso in an outward or downward motion, pushing negativity away from you.

A WAXING MOON SPELL:
A RITUAL TO PROMOTE FERTILITY

Using waxing-moon water, circle your home three times, three days before the full moon. If you have a house and yard, circle the perimeter of your property. If you live in an apartment, circling the interior of your home is fine. Be sure to sprinkle water outside the front door. Reserve about a cup of this water and add it to your bath or shower. As you bathe in it, envision what you would like to bring into your life.

A DARK MOON SPELL:
A SPELL TO TURN AWAY JEALOUSY

If others are jealous of you and either sending you bad vibes or treating you poorly because they want what you have (or what they think you have), the following spell will protect you from the detrimental effects of callous attitudes.

Dig a hole on your property. If you live in an apartment, the grounds near your building or the closest park will also do just fine. In the hole, sprinkle hot peppers, garlic, and a small portion of cooked meat, if you are able (lamb is best). Also include a cobweb or a piece of ivy, if you can find one. If you can't find either, a piece of cotton yarn (be sure to use biodegradable products) tangled up to represent a cobweb will do just fine.

Over this offering, say the following:

> Mother Hekate, the dark night queen,
> Attracts the forces seen and unseen,
> Whose bile and vitriol haunt my claims,
> Find and be caught in this web and frame.

Bury the items, turn, and walk to your home. Do not turn around.

Immediately after you do this, draw or print out a picture of an eye and hang it over your bed or in a window. Some metaphysical stores may carry evil-eye pendants, which are also quite good. This is to ensure the negativity won't return.

TWO LOVE SPELLS WITH HEKATE

Love spells are controversial among Witches. Some believe that to cast a love spell interferes with the free will of another person and is unethical. Others believe that few, if any, spells can ever take away a person's free will and that a love spell opens up attraction that already exists, even if that attraction is just a thread initially. I'm of the latter school of thought, although I tend to avoid doing love spells. They rarely bring the results the Witch is looking for, as human emotions are a complicated thing, leading to often complicated results. However, meeting my husband was the result of a love spell—one I cast with the intention of bringing the right love to me, in the form of a life mate—and I couldn't be happier with the results! As with all magick, no specific kind of spell is objectively unethical. Certain spells may be against a Witch's individual set of ethics, and for some Witches, love spells are just that. But particularly when a person's income, well-being, or support for their children is tied to a wayward lover returning, a love spell could be an extremely helpful, and ethical, thing. Humans in general long for companionship. Positive, nurturing relationships are helpful to our well-being. I personally believe love spells are a reasonable way for Witches to bring love into their lives. But just like dating, love Magick provides plentiful "oops!" moments along the way to finding the right spell and, ultimately, the right romantic situation. If you cast one, be patient and invoke your best sense of humor.

Whether or not you ever choose to cast a love spell, it's helpful to know that Hekate was often approached for help with wayward lovers, or to attract a new one. In the year 300 BCE, the poet Theocritus described a spell cast by a young woman on her neglectful lover at a Hekate shrine. This particular Witch made an offering of bay leaves, barley meal, a waxen puppet (likely of her distant beloved), and a thrice-poured libation to Hekate, among other things. Some of the wording can be found in the spell below:[9]

TO ENTICE A LOVER TO RETURN

Go to a crossroads with a bowl of salt water and a branch from an oak tree. If you cannot go to a crossroads, this working can be done inside a house, preferably in a doorway. Dip the branch in the water and use it to cleanse yourself, as if brushing lint off yourself with a roller brush. The idea is that you are removing the obstacles keeping your beloved away.

Collect nine bay leaves and set them in a pot or cauldron at your Hekate altar or in the space you have dedicated to Hekate. Take two candles of the same color—white, black, or red are preferred for this work—and bind them together with twine. (Some metaphysical or occult stores carry candles in the shape of people, usually male or female presenting, which can be very helpful in casting a spell if you or the object of your affections identifies with a specific gender. If you or your beloved do not self-identify with one or any gender, plain pillar candles are just fine. Basically, use two candles that you feel best represent you and the person you wish to attract!) If using human-shaped candles, be sure they are facing one another. Carve your initials into the candle designated for you, and your beloved's initials into the other.

Light the bay leaves and then the candles and offer the following incantation to Hekate as the smoke from the leaves rises:

> She who makes even the whelps shiver,
> On her goings to and fro,
> Where these tombs be and the red blood lives,
> May my love come home to me.

Burn the candles daily until they have burned completely down. Do not burn them unattended, particularly as the twine can be flammable. Bury the wax remains under your front doorstep. If you live in an apartment or cannot bury them beneath your front doorstep, consider putting them in a potted plant by the door.

TO ATTRACT A NEW LOVER

This spell works best not if you cast it on a specific person, but rather focus on bringing the best love match to you. It can be very tempting to focus on someone if you've got a big crush on them, but love spells are most successful if you focus on the best match. The best match for you could be someone you've never met or never really noticed!

Set a jar of honey or agave on your windowsill the night before the full moon, the night of the full moon, and the night after. On those nights, pray this spell over the jar:

As the mortals gaze upon the glowing Selene,
So may love gaze upon me.
Shining torchbearer of the dark night sky,
Bring my love to me.

Mix a spoonful of this honey or agave into your bathwater every night for thirty nights. Be sure to make an offering of the honey each night to Hekate (a small spoonful is fine). Keep the remainder of the honey to use as future offerings to Hekate or in spells in which you want to sweeten things.

TO HEAL A BROKEN HEART

This spell is the inverse of the one above. It can work healing any relationship, romantic, platonic, or otherwise, but if the spell above manifests into a relationship and that one ends up breaking your heart, this one is all the more important.

Set nine cloves of garlic on your windowsill on the night before, the night of, and the night after the dark moon. Recite the following over the garlic each night:

Dark mother, Hekate of the deep,
Heal my wounded heart.
Feast upon my tears.
Where there is cold and darkness in my heart,
Allow your fiery torches to warm it anew.

Soak one of the cloves in your bathwater each night for nine nights. After the ninth bath, take a cup of the water and throw it on the crossroads or, better yet, the cemetery. Remember not to look behind you when you walk away, giving the spirits and Hekate space to take away your sorrows.

For all of these spells, the magick is not enough. If you want your lover to return, make sure you are also working to make yourself a better partner for them when they return. If you are hoping to meet someone new or attract a person to you (although I still recommend not focusing on a single person, but rather focusing on finding the *right* person), make sure you are getting out and making the effort to meet people. If you are trying to heal from a broken heart, make sure you are taking as much space from that person as possible. This includes unfollowing them on social media.

SPELLS TO CURSE OR THWART

Cursing, the act of using magick to create harm or conflict for another person or group of people, is another area of magick that invites controversy. When I first began practicing Witchcraft, cursing was strongly discouraged. In recent years, as Witchcraft has been further partnered with fighting oppressive persons or systems, cursing is sometimes considered an act of resistance and liberation. In my view, cursing, like love spells, has its place. But like love spells, curses can also be complicated and unpredictable. In Chapter 6, we explored the necessity of placing anger in a productive place, remembering that placing a curse based in reaction can require a lot of cleanup later. Then again, you may have fully justified reasons for casting a curse, fighting something objectively harmful, no matter your level of emotional intensity around the subject.

It is not my place to say when or if someone should use any of this magick. But even if you never lay a curse in your entire life, it's good for all Witches to at least know how to do it. You never know when you're going to have to counter one, and the Witches who can best counter curses are also the ones who know how to cast them!

An easy way to call upon Hekate in a curse is to use a practice and incantation crafted especially for her. One such spell reads as follows:

> I bind them all in lead and in wax
> in water, wine, magic thread,
> and idleness and in obscurity and in ill-repute
> and in defeat and among tombs.[10]

This can be written on a biodegradable piece of paper and buried or left in a cemetery, written alongside the name of the person, organization, or situation you wish to curse. When possible, use the grave or cemetery where someone you know is buried, or else in a very old cemetery hungry for attention. If you don't have access to either, leaving the paper upside down in a glass of water and leaving the glass on an altar dedicated to either your ancestor or to Hekate will likely do the trick too.

A SPELL TO THWART AN OPPRESSOR

Magick has always had a role in disarming oppressors. Whether it's an erratic employer, a vindictive landlord, or a person of power misusing their position, the following spell will disable their ability to harm.

Take an effigy of the person (a photo from the internet is always an easy fix). Wrap the effigy in wool (black wool if possible). Speak the following prayer over the bound effigy:

> So that we may all be more confident
> In the doings of our work
> Let the oldest flock leader among [his/her/their] sheep
> Become a lamb by my hand.

Bury this effigy in the cemetery on the day of the dark moon. If you can access the cemetery at night, that's even better, though doing the work in the daytime is a fine substitute.

Note: whenever doing cemetery work, leave an offering at the gates (coins or flowers), and consider picking up any trash you see as you're leaving. Be careful not to disturb any of the graves.

A SPELL FOR PROTECTION OF THE HOME

Remember that one of Hekate's oldest primary roles was that of house and home protector.

A very old rite asking Hekate for this protection involved setting little round cakes with candles at the crossroads, as a gift sacred to both Hekate and Artemis. These were made on the thirtieth of each month, the intention being not only to please the goddesses but also to prevent spirits from invading a household.[11] Sometimes the rite included a supper with garlic, eggs, mullet, or things that might be surprising, such as *katharmata*—table scraps or other garbage sacred to Hekate.[12] These offerings and rites were deeply rooted in the hearts of people, so much so that the Church found itself trying to break up these practices even until the eleventh century CE.[13]

Consider doing a similar rite for Hekate. Leaving an offering on the thirtieth of each month will not only be a good method of magickal home protection, it will also be a good way to strengthen your connection to Hekate. Many Witches leave statues of Hekate by their front door for this reason.

When making your protection rite to Hekate, light three candles around the offering and saying the following incantation:

> Hekate, Kleidoukhos,
> Glorious keeper of the keys,
> Luminous guardian of the gates,

Protect this home from evil and threat
Of the flesh, of the spirit, of the mind.
Hail Hekate, keeper of the keys!

PROTECTION BEFORE TRAVELING

Repeat the rite above before traveling, reciting the following incantation:

Hekate, Triformis,
Luminous lady of the crossroads
Protect me as I travel these dark roads.
Shield me from evil and threat
Of the flesh, of the spirit, of the mind.
Hail Hekate! Lady of the three ways!

Look for things that remind you of Hekate when you travel (signs of keys, images of dogs, or roads where three paths meet), and offer a word of prayer and thanks. Saying the above prayer is a good way to go!

REMAINING OPEN TO LUCK

Dedicate a key to Hekate. Make an offering to her on the thirtieth of each month. On the night you make your offering, leave the key nearby, perhaps at the base of a Hekate effigy or on your altar. Carry this key with you regularly in your pocket, wallet, or purse, or on a chain around your neck.

MONEY SPELL

Basil, one of Hekate's sacred herbs, also has a history of being a great money plant. If you can procure basil essential oil, add a few drops to a base oil (such as olive, mineral, or jojoba oil). Leave the mixture on the windowsill from the new moon until the full moon. Each night, whisper over the jar of oil:

> May Hekate open the gates
> To my wealth and prosperity
> Through you, this magick oil.

Anoint yourself on your hands when doing business or interviewing for a job. Whenever the magick manifests, make an offering to Hekate.

Note: Don't apply undiluted essential oils to your skin, or take them internally. People who are pregnant or nursing should consult a physician before handling any essential oils.

Conclusion

She is a mama bird that will push you out of the nest, making you find your wings and fly. Unbeknownst to you, though, she has flown underneath to catch you should you fall. Like a bird, Hekate is a witch because she has access to all realms ... above, below, and in between.
—MARIA PALMA-DREXLER, MODERN HEKATE DEVOTEE

Witchcraft is hard. It's probably supposed to be. When I've heard people, mostly nervous non-Witches, refer to it as a dark path, I used to deny it. Now, I know it's true. But it's not a dark path because it's evil. It's dark because, unlike other spiritual paths with books and creeds and expectations, which act like highways with good lighting, signs, and billboards, Witchcraft is the unlit path through a dense forest. Sometimes we can follow a path that someone else has forged for us, but the way is largely lit by intuition and a quiet voice that gently urges us to go forward. But there will be moments when that intuition is shaky and the voice is silent.

When I left the religion of my youth and embraced Witchcraft, I thought I'd found "the answer." Witchcraft was my landing pad, my final destination. I felt I'd checked the box: now that I'd figured out what I believed spiritually, I could move on with my life and never wonder again! What I didn't read in any books nor hear in any conversations at festivals was that a crisis of faith can happen to Witches, too. There will be times when it feels like the gods are far away. We will go through periods when the world doesn't feel magickal. We may wonder why we ever started this journey. We may gaze longingly at other paths, thinking that maybe we've hit a dead end.

At least, that's where I was. I even found myself gazing jealously at the religion of my youth. I might not agree with all of the theology or any of the politics, and I might find the whole thing fully constricting, but at least there were answers . . . right? Mostly, I was just so tired. But just as good friends scoop us up when we are tired, the gods also come through just when we need them. One night toward the end of writing this book, Hekate paid a call.

A good friend phoned asking for help with a seemingly impossible situation. My husband asked if we could do magick for this friend. Feeling tired and momentarily unmagickal, I obliged. We devised a spell that would be helpful for this situation. I didn't think a lot about whether it would work, but I wanted to do something nice for our friend. Maybe it would put them in a different state of mind so they could navigate the situation more aptly—a magickal placebo is better than nothing at all.

We began with a ritual to Hekate, visiting the crossroads near our house each night, close to midnight, for the three nights surrounding a new moon. We blessed and lit some candles, and prayed to both Hekate and our ancestors in honor of our friend. We went on about our days and didn't think anything else about it.

Exactly nine days later, my husband got a call from our friend. The situation that had gripped them was gone. Obliterated. Ashes. Nothing left. There was no need to soothe our friend's nerves so that they could better navigate the situation. There was no longer any situation to navigate. Our friend was shocked and frightened, as it was their first experience with Witchcraft. My husband and I were stunned, too.

When I heard the news, I cackled. It suddenly occurred to me why Witches don't just laugh—they cackle. It's not because we're laughing at something dramatic or frightening; we cackle because of the joy in knowing that the gods and spirits can hear us, and that they do deliver, often in quite surprising ways.

It is my hope that Hekate will be that guide for you. I hope that she lights your way when it becomes hard to see the path forward. I hope that she unlocks the door to your most powerful Witch self, protects you with her hounds, helps you to make peace with your most troublesome ghosts. Above all, I hope she appears to you as gentle and loving as she has appeared to me, and that this book helped answer at least a few of your questions about her and about your path as a Witch.

Thank you for reading. May your magick be bountiful and blessed.

ACKNOWLEDGMENTS

I could not have finished this book without these people: Judika Illes and the team at Weiser Books, thank you for once again granting me this beautiful opportunity.

Thank you Jené Ashley Colvin, Lisa Anderson, and the rest of the Cauldron Squad for the Tarot readings, love, and encouragement to make this book happen.

Caitlin Abdow, Maleaha Davenport, Alanna Butler Gallagher, Gypsy Jean Cottam, Adam Forrest, Frederick Joseph, Elizabeth LaBarca, Gemma McGowan, Angelo Narcios, Christopher Penczak, "Mr. Tibbles," Misha Magdelene, Tamara Sulc, Laura Tempest Zakroff, the Novices of the Old Ways, and members of the Former Lunar Temple, thank you for your resources, support, kindness, and patience.

Sarah Bitner, Thorne Davis, Maria Palma-Drexler, Tamrha Richardson, and Wilson Joel Rios, thank you for so graciously sharing your Hekate experiences and scholarship, and *more* resources.

Thank you to my loving family: the Webers, the Gordons, and the Hoovers. Finally, thank you to my beloved husband, Brian—the greatest gift magick has ever offered.

NOTES

Epigraph

1 Hesiod, *Hesiod, the Homeric Hymns, and Homerica,* trans. by Hugh G. Evelyn-White (New York: Macmillan, 1914).

Chapter 1: Meeting Hekate

1 Stephen Ronan, ed., *The Goddess Hekate: Studies in Ancient Pagan and Christian Religion and Philosophy, Vol. 1* (Hastings, UK: Chthonios Books, 1992), 5.

2 Robert Von Rudloff, *Hekate in Ancient Greek Religion* (Victoria, BC: Horned Owl Publishing, 1999), 52.

3 Sorita d'Este and David Rankine, *Hekate Liminal Rites: A Study of the Rituals, Magic and Symbols of the Torch-Bearing Triple Goddess of the Crossroads* (London: Avalonia, 2009), 15.

4 Elicia Ann Penman, "'Toil and Trouble': Changes of Imagery to Hekate and Medea in Ovid's *Metamorphoses,*" bachelor's thesis, University of Queensland, 2014, *www.academia.edu,* 12.

5 d'Este and Rankine, *Hekate Liminal Rites,* 37.

6 Jacob Rabinowitz, *The Rotting Goddess: The Origin of the Witch in Classical Antiquity* (Brooklyn, NY: Autonomedia, 1998), 18.

7 J. E. Lowe, "Magical Hekate," in *The Goddess Hekate: Studies in Ancient Pagan and Christian Religion and Philosophy,* Vol. I., edited by Stephen Ronan (Hastings, UK: Chthonios Books, 1992), 11.

8 Daniel Ogden, *Magic, Witchcraft, and Ghosts in the Greek and Roman Worlds* (New York: Oxford University Press, 2002), 87.

9 Ogden, *Magic, Witchcraft, and Ghosts in the Greek and Roman Worlds,* 91.

10 d'Este and Rankine, *Hekate Liminal Rites,* 34.

11 d'Este and Rankine, *Hekate Liminal Rites,* 35.

12 Lowe, "Magical Hekate," 12.

13 Lowe, "Magical Hekate," 11.

14 Rick Strelan, "'Outside Are the Dogs and the Sorcerers . . .' (Revelation 22:15)," *Biblical Theology Bulletin* 33, no. 4 (November 2003), 152.

15 Sarah Iles Johnston, *Hekate Soteira: A Study of Hekate's Roles in the Chaldean Oracles and Related Literature* (Atlanta, GA: Scholars Press, 1990), 1.

16 Lowe, "Magical Hekate," 11.

17 Georg Luck, trans. *Arcana Mundi: Magic and the Occult in the Greek and Roman Worlds* (Baltimore, MD: Johns Hopkins University Press, 1985), 15.

18 Strelan, "'Outside Are the Dogs and the Sorcerers . . . ,'" 152.

19 Ronan, *The Goddess Hekate*, 5.

20 Derek Collins, *Magic in the Ancient Greek World* (Malden, MA: Blackwell Publishing, 2018), 95.

21 Von Rudloff, *Hekate in Ancient Greek Religion*, 50.

CHAPTER 2: THE WITCH IN THE FAMILY

1 William Smith, ed., *Dictionary of Greek and Roman Biography and Mythology, Vol. 2* (London: John Murray, 1890), 264.

2 J. E. Lowe, "Magical Hekate," in *The Goddess Hekate: Studies in Ancient Pagan and Christian Religion and Philosophy*, Vol. I., edited by Stephen Ronan (Hastings, UK: Chthonios Books, 1992), 11.

3 Sorita d'Este and David Rankine, *Hekate Liminal Rites: A Study of the Rituals, Magic and Symbols of the Torch-Bearing Triple Goddess of the Crossroads* (London: Avalonia, 2009), 25.

4 Georg Luck, trans. *Arcana Mundi: Magic and the Occult in the Greek and Roman Worlds* (Baltimore, MD: Johns Hopkins University Press, 1985), 9.

5 d'Este and Rankine, *Hekate Liminal Rites*, 23.

6 d'Este and Rankine, *Hekate Liminal Rites*, 24.

7 d'Este and Rankine, *Hekate Liminal Rites*, 29.

8 d'Este and Rankine, *Hekate Liminal Rites*, 24.

9 Robert Von Rudloff, *Hekate in Ancient Greek Religion* (Victoria, BC: Horned Owl Publishing, 1999), 421–428.

10 David Braund, *Greek Religion and Cults in the Black Sea Region: Goddesses in the Bosporan Kingdom from the Archaic Period to the Byzantine Era* (Cambridge, UK: Cambridge University Press, 2018), 31.

11 Lowe, "Magical Hekate," 11.

12 d'Este and Rankine, *Hekate Liminal Rites*, 16.

13 L. R. Farnell, "Hekate's Cult," in *The Goddess Hekate: Studies in Ancient Pagan and Christian Religion and Philosophy*, Vol. 1., edited by Stephen Ronan (Hastings, UK: Chthonios Books, 1992), 21.

14 Braund, *Greek Religion and Cults in the Black Sea Region*, 15.

15 d'Este and Rankine, *Hekate Liminal Rites*, 25.

16 d'Este and Rankine, *Hekate Liminal Rites*, 28.

17 d'Este and Rankine, *Hekate Liminal Rites*, 38.

18 Luck, *Arcana Mundi*, 3.

19 d'Este and Rankine, *Hekate Liminal Rites*, 42.

20 Luck, *Arcana Mundi*, 26.

21 Eleni Pachoumi, *The Concepts of the Divine in the Greek Magical Papyri* (Tubingen, Germany: Mohr Siebeck, 2017), 130.

22 d'Este and Rankine, *Hekate Liminal Rites*, 41.

23 Pachoumi, *The Concepts of the Divine in the Greek Magical Papyri*, 130.

24 Von Rudloff, *Hekate in Ancient Greek Religion*, 17.

25 Joan Marler, "An Archaeomythological Investigation of the Gorgon," *ReVision* 25, no. 1 (2002), 4.

26 Marler, "An Archaeomythological Investigation of the Gorgon," 6.

27 Rick Strelan, "'Outside Are the Dogs and the Sorcerers . . .' (Revelation 22:15)," *Biblical Theology Bulletin* 33, no. 4 (November 2003), 155.

28 d'Este and Rankine, *Hekate Liminal Rites*, 62.

29 Sarah Iles Johnston, *Hekate Soteira: A Study of Hekate's Roles in the Chaldean Oracles and Related Literature* (Atlanta, GA: Scholars Press, 1990), 123.

30 Marler, "An Archaeomythological Investigation of the Gorgon," 8.

31 W. K. C. Guthrie, *The Greeks and Their Gods* (Boston: Beacon Press, 1950), 228.

CHAPTER 3: TORCHBEARER: THE LIGHT IN THE DARK

1 Translation by Stephen Radt, retrieved from *cf.hum.uva.nl/narratology.*

2 Gregory Nagy, trans. "Homeric Hymn to Demeter," *www.uh.edu.*

3 Carol M. Mooney, "Hekate: Her Role and Character in Greek Literature from before the Fifth Century B.C.," PhD diss., McMaster University, 1971, 22.

4 Randy P. Conner, "Come, Hekate, I Call You to My Sacred Chants," *www.academia.edu,* 3.

5 Conner, "Come, Hekate," 3.

6 Conner, "Come, Hekate," 3.

7 Geoffrey Miles, "Ramfeezled Hizzies and Arachnoid Hags: Baxter, Burns, and the Muse," *Journal of New Zealand Literature* 30 (2012), 86.

8 Attilio Mastrocinque, *Kronos, Shiva, & Asklepios: Studies in Magical Gems and Religions of the Roman Empire* (Philadelphia: American Philosophical Society, 2011), 116.

9 Miles, "Ramfeezled Hizzies and Arachnoid Hags," 87.

10 Jacob Rabinowitz, *The Rotting Goddess: The Origin of the Witch in Classical Antiquity* (Brooklyn, NY: Autonomedia, 1998), 44.

11 Dimitar Vasilev Georgieff, "About Melinoe and Hekate Trimorphis in the Bronze Tablet from the Town of Pergamon," *www.academia.edu,* 1.

12 Conner, "Come, Hekate," 3.

13 Stephen Ronan, ed., *The Goddess Hekate: Studies in Ancient Pagan and Christian Religion and Philosophy, Vol. I* (Hastings, UK: Chthonios Books, 1992), 116.

14 Charlene Spretnak, *Lost Goddesses of Early Greece: A Collection of Pre-Hellenic Myths* (Boston: Beacon Press, 1992), 76.

15 Jerusha Behari, "Ambivalent Goddesses in Patriarchies: A Comparative Study of Hekate in Ancient Greek and Roman Religion, and Kali in Contemporary Hinduism," PhD diss., University of KwaZulu-Natal, 2011, 166.

16 Mary Elizabeth Coen, "The Triple Goddess Myth," Goddess Meca, September 9, 2013, *www.goddessmeca.com.*

17 William James Harvey, "Reflections on the Enigmatic Goddess: The Origins of Hekate and the Development of Her Character to the End of the Fifth Century B.C.," master's thesis, University of Otago, 2013, 104.

18 Harvey, "Reflections on the Enigmatic Goddess," 126.

19 Behari, "Ambivalent Goddesses in Patriarchies," 168.

20 Edward P. Butler, "Flower of Fire: Hekate in the *Chaldean Oracles*," in *Bearing Torches: A Devotional Anthology for Hekate*, edited by Sannion and the editorial board of the Bibliotheca Alexandrina (Eugene, OR: Bibliotheca Alexandrina, 2009), 7.

21 Alexander Hollmann, "A Curse Tablet from the Circus at Antioch," *Zeitschrift für Papyrologie und Epigraphik* 145 (2003), 78.

22 L. R. Farnell, "Hekate's Cult," in *The Goddess Hekate: Studies in Ancient Pagan and Christian Religion and Philosophy, Vol. 1*, edited by Stephen Ronan (Hastings, UK: Chthonios Books, 1992), 22–23.

23 Butler, "Flower of Fire," 16.

24 Shelly M. Nixon, "Hekate: Bringer of Light," California Institute of Integral Studies, 2013, 8.

25 Nixon, "Hekate: Bringer of Light," 10.

26 Rabinowitz, *The Rotting Goddess*, 25.

27 Robert Von Rudloff, *Hekate in Ancient Greek Religion* (Victoria, BC: Horned Owl Publishing, 1999), 26.

28 Behari, "Ambivalent Goddesses in Patriarchies," 78.

29 Harvey, "Reflections on the Enigmatic Goddess," 26.

30 Sorita d'Este and David Rankine, *Hekate Liminal Rites: A Study of the Rituals, Magic and Symbols of the Torch-Bearing Triple Goddess of the Crossroads* (London: Avalonia, 2009), 38.

31 Elicia Ann Penman, "'Toil and Trouble': Changes of Imagery to Hekate and Medea in Ovid's *Metamorphoses*," bachelor's thesis, University of Queensland, 2014, 15.

32 Butler, "Flower of Fire," 7.

CHAPTER 4: RITUAL, MAGICK, AND THE CROSSROADS

1 Tim Ward, "Hekate at Lagina and Çatalhöyük," in *Bearing Torches: A Devotional Anthology for Hekate*, edited by Sannion and the editorial board of the Bibliotheca Alexandrina (Eugene, OR: Bibliotheca Alexandrina, 2009), 85.

2 Fritz Graf and Sarah Iles Johnston, *Ritual Texts for the Afterlife: Orpheus and the Bacchic Gold Tablets* (New York: Routledge, 2013), Appendix 2, Note 5.

3 Carol M. Mooney, "Hekate: Her Role and Character in Greek Literature from before the Fifth Century B.C.," PhD diss., McMaster University, 1971, 74.

4 Rick Strelan, "'Outside Are the Dogs and the Sorcerers . . .' (Revelation 22:15)." *Biblical Theology Bulletin* 33, no. 4 (November 2003), 154.

5 Sarah Iles Johnston, *Hekate Soteira: A Study of Hekate's Roles in the Chaldean Oracles and Related Literature* (Atlanta, GA: Scholars Press, 1990), 217.

6 Marie-Louise Thomsen, "Witchcraft and Magic in Ancient Mesopotamia," in *Witchcraft and Magic in Europe, Vol. 1*, edited by Bengt Ankarloo and Stuart Clark (Philadelphia: University of Pennsylvania Press, 2001), 63–64.

7 Sarah Iles Johnston, "Crossroads," *ZPE 88* (1991), 224.

8 Stephen Ronan, ed., *The Goddess Hekate: Studies in Ancient Pagan and Christian Religion and Philosophy, Vol. 1* (Hastings, UK: Chthonios Books, 1992), 6.

9 Martin P. Nilsson, *Greek Folk Religion* (New York: Columbia University Press, 1971), 80.

10 Strelan, "'Outside Are the Dogs and the Sorcerers . . .,'" 154.

11 Strelan, "'Outside Are the Dogs and the Sorcerers . . .,'" 154.

12 Johnston, *Hekate Soteira*, 220.

13 Jacob Rabinowitz, *The Rotting Goddess: The Origin of the Witch in Classical Antiquity* (Brooklyn, NY: Autonomedia, 1998), 23.

14 Johnston, *Hekate Soteira*, 74.

15 Sorita d'Este and David Rankine, *Hekate Liminal Rites: A Study of the Rituals, Magic and Symbols of the Torch-Bearing Triple Goddess of the Crossroads* (London: Avalonia, 2009), 224.

16 Johnston, *Hekate Soteira*, 217.

17 Johnston, *Hekate Soteira*, 217, 222.

18 Johnston, *Hekate Soteira*, 223.

19 Sarah Iles Johnston, *Restless Dead: Encounters between the Living and the Dead in Ancient Greece* (Oakland: University of California Press, 1999), 61.

20 Johnston, *Hekate Soteira*, 224.

21 Pierre de Lancre, *On the Inconstancy of Witches: Pierre de Lancre's Tableau de l'inconstance des mauvais anges et demons (1612)*, edited and translated by Gerhild Scholz Williams et al. (Tempe: Arizona Center for Medieval and Renaissance Studies, 2006), 69–70.

22 W. K. C. Guthrie, *The Greeks and Their Gods* (Boston: Beacon Press, 1950), 222.

23 d'Este and Rankine, *Hekate Liminal Rites*, 223.

24 d'Este and Rankine, *Hekate Liminal Rites*, 223.

25 Guthrie, *The Greeks and Their Gods*, 221.

26 Guthrie, *The Greeks and Their Gods*, 222.

27 Johnston, *Restless Dead*, 60.

28 Guthrie, *The Greeks and Their Gods*, 222.

29 Theresa Reed's *Astrology for Real Life* is an excellent resource for astrological correspondences. For ocean tide tables, I recommend Annwyn Avalon's *Water Witchcraft*.

30 de Lancre, *On the Inconstancy of Witches*, 70.

31 Rabinowitz, *The Rotting Goddess*, 64.

CHAPTER 5: GODDESS OF GHOSTS

1 Apollonios Rhodios, *The Argonautika*, translated by Peter Green (Berkeley: University of California Press, 2008), 135.

2 Dimitar Vasilev Georgieff, "About Melinoe and Hekate Trimorphis in the Bronze Tablet from the Town of Pergamon," *www.academia.edu*, 3.

3 Simon Price, *Religions of the Ancient Greeks* (Cambridge, UK: Cambridge University Press, 2006), 101.

4 Jerusha Behari, "Ambivalent Goddesses in Patriarchies: A Comparative Study of Hekate in Ancient Greek and Roman Religion, and Kali in Contemporary Hinduism," PhD diss., University of KwaZulu-Natal, 2011, 169–170.

5 Sarah Iles Johnston, *Hekate Soteira: A Study of Hekate's Roles in the Chaldean Oracles and Related Literature* (Atlanta, GA: Scholars Press, 1990), 7.

6 Johnston, *Hekate Soteira*, 8.

7 Charlene Spretnak, *Lost Goddesses of Early Greece: A Collection of Pre-Hellenic Myths* (Boston: Beacon Press, 1992), 76.

8 J. E. Lowe, "Magical Hekate," in *The Goddess Hekate: Studies in Ancient Pagan and Christian Religion and Philosophy, Vol. 1*, edited by Stephen Ronan (Hastings, UK: Chthonios Books, 1992), 12.

9 Lowe, "Magical Hekate," 14.

10 Martin P. Nilsson, *Greek Folk Religion* (New York: Columbia University Press, 1971), 112.

11 Semni Karouzou, "An Underworld Scene on a Black-Figured Lekythos," *The Journal of Hellenic Studies* 92 (1972), 72.

12 Derek Collins, *Magic in the Ancient Greek World* (Malden, MA: Blackwell Publishing, 2018), 37.

13 Sarah Iles Johnston, *Restless Dead: Encounters Between the Living and the Dead in Ancient Greece* (Oakland: University of California Press, 1999), 30–31.

14 L. R. Farnell, "Hekate's Cult," in *The Goddess Hekate: Studies in Ancient Pagan and Christian Religion and Philosophy, Vol. 1,* edited by Stephen Ronan (Hastings, UK: Chthonios Books, 1992), 31–32.

15 William James Harvey, "Reflections on the Enigmatic Goddess: The Origins of Hekate and the Development of Her Character to the End of the Fifth Century B.C.," master's thesis, University of Otago, 2013, 5.

16 Behari, "Ambivalent Goddesses in Patriarchies," 84.

17 *The Real Story of Halloween,* directed by Luke Ellis, 2010, A&E.

18 Harvey, "Reflections on the Enigmatic Goddess," 132.

19 Rick Strelan, "'Outside Are the Dogs and the Sorcerers . . .' (Revelation 22:15)." *Biblical Theology Bulletin* 33, no. 4 (November 2003), 154.

20 Strelan, "'Outside Are the Dogs and the Sorcerers . . . ,'" 155.

21 Joan Marler, "An Archaeomythological Investigation of the Gorgon." *ReVision* 25, no. 1 (2002), 15.

22 Farnell, "Hekate's Cult," 24.

23 Strelan, "'Outside Are the Dogs and the Sorcerers . . . ,'" 148.

24 Strelan, "'Outside Are the Dogs and the Sorcerers . . . ,'" 151.

25 Price, *Religions of the Ancient Greeks,* 101.

26 Alexander Hollmann, "A Curse Tablet from the Circus at Antioch." *Zeitschrift für Papyrologie und Epigraphik* 145 (2003), 77.

27 Price, *Religions of the Ancient Greeks,* 101.

28 Collins, *Magic in the Ancient Greek World,* 10.

29 Johnston, *Restless Dead,* 31.

30 Price, *Religions of the Ancient Greeks,* 101–102.

31 Jessica Laura Lamont, "A New Commercial Curse Tablet from Classical Athens," *Zeitschrift für Papyrologie und Epigraphik* 196 (2015), 159.

32 Lamont, "A New Commercial Curse Tablet from Classical Athens," 173.

33 Interpretation is mine. Based on translation found in Lamont, "A New Commercial Curse Tablet from Classical Athens," 162.

34 Lamont, "A New Commercial Curse Tablet from Classical Athens," 167.

35 Price, *Religions of the Ancient Greeks,* 101.

36 Lamont, "A New Commercial Curse Tablet from Classical Athens," 173.

37 Lamont, "A New Commercial Curse Tablet from Classical Athens," 160.

38 Lamont, "A New Commercial Curse Tablet from Classical Athens," 160.

39 Shakespeare's Macbeth, Act 2, Scene 1, Verses 49–54.

40 For more information, see *Lifting the Veil* by Janet Farrar and Gavin Bone.

CHAPTER 6: THE DANGEROUS GODDESS AND THE DANGEROUS WITCH

1 Aleister Crowley, *Moonchild* (New York: Red Wheel/Weiser, 1970), 187.

2 Pierre de Lancre, *On the Inconstancy of Witches: Pierre de Lancre's Tableau de l'inconstance des mauvais anges et demons (1612),* edited and translated by Gerhild Scholz Williams et al. (Tempe: Arizona Center for Medieval and Renaissance Studies, 2006), 69.

3 For more information, see *Magic, Witchcraft, and Ghosts in the Greek and Roman Worlds* by Daniel Ogden.

4 Sorita d'Este and David Rankine, *Hekate Liminal Rites: A Study of the Rituals, Magic and Symbols of the Torch-Bearing Triple Goddess of the Crossroads* (London: Avalonia, 2009), 237.

5 Daniel Ogden, *Magic, Witchcraft, and Ghosts in the Greek and Roman Worlds* (New York: Oxford University Press, 2002), 240.

6 Apollonius Rhodius, "Argonautica Book 4," translated by R. C. Seaton, Theoi Project, 2017, *www.theoi.com,* section 1191.

7 Apollonius Rhodius, "Argonautica Book 4," section 1659.

8 Rendition taken from Diodorus, in Ogden, *Magic, Witchcraft, and Ghosts in the Greek and Roman Worlds,* 78–79.

9 Seneca, *Medea,* translated by Frederick Ahl (Ithaca, NY: Cornell University Press, 1986), Act One, Verses 1–20.

10 Sarah Iles Johnston, *Hekate Soteira: A Study of Hekate's Roles in the Chaldean Oracles and Related Literature* (Atlanta, GA: Scholars Press, 1990), 153.

11 John Pollard, *Seers, Shrines, and Sirens: The Greek Religious Revolution in the Sixth Century B.C.* (London: Unwin University Books, 1965), 61.

12 Semni Karouzou, "An Underworld Scene on a Black-Figured Lekythos," *The Journal of Hellenic Studies* 92 (1972), 66.

13 Eleni Pachoumi, *The Concepts of the Divine in the Greek Magical Papyri* (Tubingen, Germany: Mohr Siebeck, 2017), 21.

14 Karouzou, "An Underworld Scene on a Black-Figured Lekythos," 67.

15 Johnston, *Hekate Soteira*, 222.

16 Ovid, *Heroides*. 6.83–94, in Ogden, *Magic, Witchcraft, and Ghosts in the Greek and Roman Worlds,* 126.

CHAPTER 7: KEEPER OF THE KEYS

1 Apollonius Rhodius, "Argonautica Book 4," trans. R. C. Seaton, Theoi Project, 2017, *www.theoi.com*, section 55.

2 Jerusha Behari, "Ambivalent Goddesses in Patriarchies: A Comparative Study of Hekate in Ancient Greek and Roman Religion, and Kali in Contemporary Hinduism," PhD diss., University of KwaZulu-Natal, 2011, 69.

3 Sarah Iles Johnston, "Riders in the Sky" Cavalier Gods and Theurgic Salvation in the Second Century A.D.," *Classical Philology, Vol. 87, No. 4 (1992),* 318–319.

4 Sarah Iles Johnston, *Hekate Soteira: A Study of Hekate's Roles in the Chaldean Oracles and Related Literature* (Atlanta, GA: Scholars Press, 1990), 21.

5 Robert Von Rudloff, *Hekate in Ancient Greek Religion* (Victoria, BC: Horned Owl Publishing, 1999), 51.

6 William James Harvey, "Reflections on the Enigmatic Goddess: The Origins of Hekate and the Development of Her Character to the End of the Fifth Century B.C.," master's thesis, University of Otago, 2013, 45.

7 Johnston, *Hekate Soteira,* 42.

8 Carol M. Mooney, "Hekate: Her Role and Character in Greek Literature from before the Fifth Century B.C.," PhD diss., McMaster University, 1971, 13.

9 Mooney, "Hekate," 15, Note 42.

10 Rick Strelan, "'Outside Are the Dogs and the Sorcerers . . .' (Revelation 22:15)," *Biblical Theology Bulletin* 33, no. 4 (November 2003), 154.

11 Strelan, "'Outside Are the Dogs and the Sorcerers . . . ,'" 151.

12 Strelan, "'Outside Are the Dogs and the Sorcerers . . . ,'" 148.

13 Jacob Rabinowitz, *The Rotting Goddess: The Origin of the Witch in Classical Antiquity* (Brooklyn, NY: Autonomedia, 1998), 24.

14 L. R. Farnell, "Hekate in Art," in *The Goddess Hekate: Studies in Ancient Pagan and Christian Religion and Philosophy, Vol. 1,* edited by Stephen Ronan (Hastings, UK: Chthonios Books, 1992), 36–56; and Strelan, "'Outside Are the Dogs and the Sorcerers . . . ,'" 153.

15 Semni Karouzou, "An Underworld Scene on a Black-Figured Lekythos," *The Journal of Hellenic Studies* 92 (1972), 65.

16 Rabinowitz, *The Rotting Goddess,* 24.

17 Strelan, "'Outside Are the Dogs and the Sorcerers . . . ,'" 153.

18 Johnston, *Hekate Soteira,* 2.

19 Johnston, *Hekate Soteira,* 14.

20 Johnston, *Hekate Soteira,* 21.

21 Johnston, *Hekate Soteira,* 39, 48.

22 Johnston, *Hekate Soteira,* 38.

23 Edward P. Butler, "Flower of Fire: Hekate in the *Chaldean Oracles,*" in *Bearing Torches: A Devotional Anthology for Hekate,* edited by Sannion and the editorial board of the Bibliotheca Alexandrina (Eugene OR: Bibliotheca Alexandrina, 2009), 20.

24 Butler, "Flower of Fire," 24.

25 Adam Forrest, "The Orphic Hymn to Hekatê," Hermetic Fellowship, last updated September 22, 1998, *www.hermeticfellowship.org.*

26 Inspired by Ovid's *Metamorphoses.*

27 Inspired by piece from H. D. Betz, *The Greek Magical Papyri in Translation: Including the Demotic Spells,* 2nd edition (Chicago: University of Chicago, 1992), 85.

CHAPTER 8: MOTHER, FOSTER MOTHER, AND FERTILITY GODDESS

1 Elicia Ann Penman, "'Toil and Trouble': Changes of Imagery to Hekate and Medea in Ovid's *Metamorphoses,*" bachelor's thesis, University of Queensland, 2014, 12.

2 Randy P. Conner, "Come, Hekate, I Call You to My Sacred Chants," *www.academia.edu,* 13.

3 Jean Shinoda Bolen, *Goddesses in Everywoman: Powerful Archetypes in Women's Lives* (New York: Harper and Row, 1984), 197.

4 John Pollard, *Seers, Shrines, and Sirens: The Greek Religious Revolution in the Sixth Century B.C.* (London: Unwin University Books, 1965), 67–69.

5 Simon Price, *Religions of the Ancient Greeks* (Cambridge, UK: Cambridge University Press, 2006), 19.

6 Bolen, *Goddesses in Everywoman*, 219.

7 Jerusha Behari, "Ambivalent Goddesses in Patriarchies: A Comparative Study of Hekate in Ancient Greek and Roman Religion, and Kali in Contemporary Hinduism," PhD diss., University of KwaZulu-Natal, 2011, 109.

8 Behari, "Ambivalent Goddesses in Patriarchies," 110–111.

9 Pollard, *Seers, Shrines, and Sirens*, 75.

10 Charlene Spretnak, *Lost Goddesses of Early Greece: A Collection of Pre-Hellenic Myths* (Boston: Beacon Press, 1992), 76.

11 Pollard, *Seers, Shrines, and Sirens*, 75.

12 Robert Von Rudloff, *Hekate in Ancient Greek Religion* (Victoria, BC: Horned Owl Publishing, 1999), 450–452.

13 Jacob Rabinowitz, *The Rotting Goddess: The Origin of the Witch in Classical Antiquity* (Brooklyn, NY: Autonomedia, 1998), 17.

14 Pollard, *Seers, Shrines, and Sirens*, 61.

15 Semni Karouzou, "An Underworld Scene on a Black-Figured Lekythos," *The Journal of Hellenic Studies* 92 (1972), 67.

16 Karouzou, "An Underworld Scene on a Black-Figured Lekythos," 69.

17 L. R. Farnell, "Hekate's Cult," in *The Goddess Hekate: Studies in Ancient Pagan and Christian Religion and Philosophy, Vol. 1,* edited by Stephen Ronan (Hastings, UK: Chthonios Books, 1992), 23.

18 Rabinowitz, *The Rotting Goddess*, 19.

19 Sorita d'Este and David Rankine, *Hekate Liminal Rites: A Study of the Rituals, Magic and Symbols of the Torch-Bearing Triple Goddess of the Crossroads* (London: Avalonia, 2009), 42.

20 d'Este and Rankine, *Hekate Liminal Rites*, 40.

21 Pollard, *Seers, Shrines, and Sirens*, 75.

22 Hesiod, *Theogony* 440–452, "Greek Texts & Translations," Perseus Project at University of Chicago, 1.

23 Inspired by Hesiod, *Theogony* 416–420.

CHAPTER 9: HEKATE'S GRIMOIRE

1 Herbert Weir Smyth, trans., *Aeschylus in Two Volumes, Vol. 1* (London: William Heinemann, 1922), 69.

2 Georg Luck, trans., *Arcana Mundi: Magic and the Occult in the Greek and Roman Worlds* (Baltimore, MD: Johns Hopkins University Press, 1985), 25.

3 Eleni Pachoumi, *The Concepts of the Divine in the Greek Magical Papyri* (Tubingen, Germany: Mohr Siebeck, 2017), 6.

4 Rick Strelan, "'Outside Are the Dogs and the Sorcerers . . .' (Revelation 22:15)," *Biblical Theology Bulletin* 33, no. 4 (November 2003): 153.

5 Strelan, "'Outside Are the Dogs and the Sorcerers . . . ,'" 153.

6 Strelan, "'Outside Are the Dogs and the Sorcerers . . . ,'" 153.

7 Strelan, "'Outside Are the Dogs and the Sorcerers . . . ,'" 153.

8 Full translations can be found in Stephen Ronan's *The Goddess Hekate: Studies in Ancient Pagan Religion and Christian Philosophy Vol. 1.*

9 Strelan, "'Outside Are the Dogs and the Sorcerers . . . ,'" 153.

10 Jessica Laura Lamont, "A New Commercial Curse Tablet from Classical Athens," *Zeitschrift für Papyrologie und Epigraphik* 196 (2015), 173.

11 L. R. Farnell, "Hekate's Cult," in *The Goddess Hekate: Studies in Ancient Pagan and Christian Religion and Philosophy, Vol. 1,* edited by Stephen Ronan (Hastings, UK: Chthonios Books, 1992), 27.

12 K. F. Smith, "Hekate's Suppers," in *The Goddess Hekate: Studies in Ancient Pagan and Christian Religion and Philosophy, Vol. 1,* edited by Stephen Ronan (Hastings, UK: Chthonios Books, 1992), 59.

13 Smith, "Hekate's Suppers," 61.

BIBLIOGRAPHY

Armand, Khi. *Deliverance! Hoodoo Spells of Uncrossing, Healing, and Protection.* Forestville, CA: Missionary Independent Spiritual Church, 2015.

Avalon, Annwyn. *Water Witchcraft: Magic and Lore from the Celtic Tradition.* Newburyport, MA: Weiser Books, 2019.

Behari, Jerusha. "Ambivalent Goddesses in Patriarchies: A Comparative Study of Hekate in Ancient Greek and Roman Religion, and Kali in Contemporary Hinduism." PhD diss., University of KwaZulu-Natal, 2011, *researchspace.ukzn.ac.za.*

Betz, H.D. *The Greek Magical Papyri in Translation: Including the Demotic Spells,* 2nd edition. Chicago: University of Chicago, 1992.

Blackthorn, Amy. *Sacred Smoke: Clear Away Negative Energies and Purify Body, Mind, and Spirit.* Newburyport, MA: Weiser Books, 2019.

Bolen, Jean Shinoda. *Goddesses in Everywoman: Powerful Archetypes in Women's Lives.* New York: Harper and Row, 1984.

Braund, David. *Greek Religion and Cults in the Black Sea Region: Goddesses in the Bosporan Kingdom from the Archaic Period to the Byzantine Era.* Cambridge, UK: Cambridge University Press, 2018.

Butler, Edward P. "Flower of Fire: Hekate in the *Chaldean Oracles,*" in *Bearing Torches: A Devotional Anthology for Hekate,* edited by Sannion and the editorial board of the Bibliotheca

Alexandrina. Eugene, OR: Bibliotheca Alexandrina, 2009, 140–157.

Coen, Mary Elizabeth. "The Triple Goddess Myth." Goddess Meca, September 9, 2013, *www.goddessmeca.com.*

Coleridge, Edward P. *The Plays of Euripides, Vol. 1.* London: George Bell and Sons, 1906.

Collins, Derek. *Magic in the Ancient Greek World.* Malden, MA: Blackwell Publishing, 2018.

Conner, Randy P. "Come, Hekate, I Call You to My Sacred Chants." *www.academia.edu.*

Cousland, J. R. C. "The Much Suffering Eye in Antioch's House of the Evil Eye: Is It Mithraic?" *Religious Studies and Theology* 24, no. 1 (2005): 61–74.

Crowley, Aleister. *Moonchild.* New York: Red Wheel Weiser, 1970.

de Lancre, Pierre. *On the Inconstancy of Witches: Pierre de Lancre's Tableau de l'inconstance des mauvais anges et demons (1612).* Edited and translated by Gerhild Scholz Williams et al. Tempe: Arizona Center for Medieval and Renaissance Studies, 2006.

d'Este, Sorita, and David Rankine. *Hekate Liminal Rites: A Study of the Rituals, Magic and Symbols of the Torch-Bearing Triple Goddess of the Crossroads.* London: Avalonia, 2009.

Farnell, L. R. "Hekate's Cult," in Ronan, Stephen, ed. *The Goddess Hekate: Studies in Ancient Pagan and Christian Religions and Philosophy, Vol. 1.* Hastings, UK: Chthonios Books, 1992, 17–35.

Farnell, L. R. "Hekate in Art," in Ronan, Stephen, ed. *The Goddess Hekate: Studies in Ancient Pagan and Christian Religion and Philosophy, Vol. 1.* Hastings, UK: Chthonios Books, 1992, 36–56.

Farrar, Janet, and Gavin Bone. *Lifting the Veil: A Witches' Guide to Trance-Prophesy, Drawing Down the Moon, and Ecstatic Ritual.* Portland, OR: Acorn Guild Press, 2016.

Forrest, Adam. "The Orphic Hymn to Hekatê." Hermetic Fellowship, last updated September 22, 1998, *www.hermeticfellowship.org.*

Georgieff, Dimitar Vasilev. "About Melinoe and Hekate Trimorphis in the Bronze Tablet from the Town of Pergamon." *www.academia.edu.*

Graf, Fritz, and Sarah Iles Johnston. *Ritual Texts for the Afterlife: Orpheus and the Bacchic Gold Tablets.* New York: Routledge, 2013.

Guthrie, W. K. C. *The Greeks and Their Gods.* Boston: Beacon Press, 1950.

Harvey, William James. "Reflections on the Enigmatic Goddess: The Origins of Hekate and the Development of Her Character to the End of the Fifth Century B.C." Master's thesis, University of Otago, 2013. *ourarchive.otago.ac.nz.*

Heinemann, W. *Aeschylus in Two Volumes, Vol. 1.* London: William Heinemann, 1922.

Hesiod. *Hesiod, the Homeric Hymns, and Homerica.* Translated by Hugh G. Evelyn-White. New York: Macmillan, 1914.

Hollmann, Alexander. "A Curse Tablet from the Circus at Antioch." *Zeitschrift für Papyrologie und Epigraphik* 145 (2003): 67–82.

Johnston, Sarah Iles. "Crossroads," *ZPE 88,* 1991. *www.uni-koeln.de.*

Johnston, Sarah Iles. *Hekate Soteira: A Study of Hekate's Roles in the Chaldean Oracles and Related Literature.* Atlanta, GA: Scholars Press, 1990.

Johnston, Sarah Iles. *Restless Dead: Encounters Between the Living and the Dead in Ancient Greece.* Oakland: University of California Press, 1999.

Johnston, Sarah Iles. "Riders in the Sky: Cavalier Gods and Theurgic Salvation in the Second Century, A.D." *Classical Philology* 87, no. 2 (1992): 303–321.

Karouzou, Semni. "An Underworld Scene on a Black-Figured Lekythos." *The Journal of Hellenic Studies* 92 (1972): 64–73.

Lamont, Jessica Laura. "A New Commercial Curse Tablet from Classical Athens." *Zeitschrift für Papyrologie und Epigraphik* 196 (2015): 159–174.

Lowe, J. E. "Magical Hekate," in Ronan, Stephen, ed. *The Goddess Hekate: Studies in Ancient Pagan and Christian Religion and Philosophy, Vol. 1.* Hastings, UK: Chthonios Books, 1992, 11–16.

Luck, Georg, trans. *Arcana Mundi: Magic and the Occult in the Greek and Roman Worlds.* Baltimore, MD: Johns Hopkins University Press, 1985.

Marler, Joan. "An Archaeomythological Investigation of the Gorgon." *ReVision* 25, no. 1 (2002): 15–23.

Mastrocinque, Attilio. *Kronos, Shiva, & Asklepios: Studies in Magical Gems and Religions of the Roman Empire.* Philadelphia: American Philosophical Society, 2011.

Miles, Geoffrey. "Ramfeezled Hizzies and Arachnoid Hags: Baxter, Burns, and the Muse." *Journal of New Zealand Literature* 30 (2012): 74–97.

Miller, Colin. "The Imperial Cult in the Pauline Cities of Asia Minor and Greece." *Catholic Biblical Quarterly* 72, no. 2 (2010): 314–332.

Mooney, Carol M. "Hekate: Her Role and Character in Greek Literature from before the Fifth Century B.C." PhD diss., McMaster University, 1971. *macsphere.mcmaster.ca.*

Nagy, Gregory, trans. "Homeric Hymn to Demeter." *www.uh.edu.*

Nilsson, Martin P. *Greek Folk Religion*. New York: Columbia University Press, 1971.

Nixon, Shelly M. "Hekate: Bringer of Light." California Institute of Integral Studies, 2013. *www.researchgate.net*.

Ogden, Daniel. *Magic, Witchcraft, and Ghosts in the Greek and Roman Worlds*. New York: Oxford University Press, 2002.

Pachoumi, Eleni. *The Concepts of the Divine in the Greek Magical Papyri*. Tubingen, Germany: Mohr Siebeck, 2017.

Penman, Elicia Ann. "'Toil and Trouble': Changes of Imagery to Hekate and Medea in Ovid's *Metamorphoses*." Bachelor's thesis, University of Queensland, 2014. *www.academia.edu*.

Penzcak, Christopher. *The Mighty Dead*. Salem, NH: Copper Cauldron Publishing, 2013

Pollard, John. *Seers, Shrines, and Sirens: The Greek Religious Revolution in the Sixth Century B.C.* London: Unwin University Books, 1965.

Price, Simon. *Religions of the Ancient Greeks*. Cambridge, UK: Cambridge University Press, 2006.

Rabinowitz, Jacob. *The Rotting Goddess: The Origin of the Witch in Classical Antiquity*. Brooklyn, NY: Autonomedia, 1998.

Ellis, Luke, dir. *The Real Story of Halloween*. A&E, 2010.

Reed, Theresa. *Astrology for Real Life: A Workbook for Beginners*. Newburyport, MA: Weiser Books, 2019.

Rhodios, Apollonios. *The Argonautika*. Translated by Peter Green. Berkeley: University of California Press, 2008.

Rhodius, Appollonius. *Argonautica*. Translated by R. C. Seaton. Theoi Project, 2017, *www.theoi.com*.

Ronan, Stephen, ed. *The Goddess Hekate: Studies in Ancient Pagan and Christian Religion and Philosophy, Vol. 1*. Hastings, UK: Chthonios Books, 1992.

Seneca. *Medea*. Translated by Frederick Ahl. Ithaca, NY: Cornell University Press, 1986.

Shakespeare, William. *Macbeth*. Oxford, UK: Oxford University Press, 2009.

Smith, K. F. "Hekate's Suppers," in Ronan, Stephen, ed. *The Goddess Hekate: Studies in Ancient Pagan and Christian Religion and Philosophy, Vol. 1*. Hastings, UK: Chthonios Books, 1992, 57–64.

Smith, Kathryn M. "Hekate: A Symbol of the Dangers of Feminine Knowledge in Euripides." Master's thesis, University of Kansas, 2016. *kuscholarworks.ku.edu*.

Smith, William, ed. *Dictionary of Greek and Roman Biography and Mythology, Vol. 2*. London: John Murray, Albemare Street. 1890.

Smyth, Herbert Weir, trans. *Aeschylus in Two Volumes, Vol. 1*. London: William Heinemann, 1922.

Strelan, Rick. "'Outside Are the Dogs and the Sorcerers . . .' (Revelation 22:15)." *Biblical Theology Bulletin* 33, no. 4 (November 2003): 148–157.

Spretnak, Charlene. *Lost Goddesses of Early Greece: A Collection of Pre-Hellenic Myths*. Boston: Beacon Press, 1992.

Thomsen, Marie-Louise. "Witchcraft and Magic in Ancient Mesopotamia." In *Witchcraft and Magic in Europe, Vol. 1*, edited by Bengt Ankarloo and Stuart Clark. Philadelphia: University of Pennsylvania Press, 2001.

Von Rudloff, Robert. *Hekate in Ancient Greek Religion*. Victoria, BC: Horned Owl Publishing, 1999.

Ward, Tim. "Hekate at Lagina and Çatalhöyük," in *Bearing Torches: A Devotional Anthology for Hekate*, edited by Sannion and the editorial board of the Bibliotheca Alexandrina. Eugene, OR: Bibliotheca Alexandrina, 2009, 84–96.

ABOUT THE AUTHOR

Courtney Weber is a priestess, witch, author, and tarot adviser. She is the author of *Brigid, Tarot for One,* and *The Morrigan,* and the designer of Tarot of the Boroughs, a modern tarot deck set in New York City. She cohosts the podcast *That Witch Life.* Follow her at *courtneyaweber.com* and on Instagram @thecocowitch.

TO OUR READERS